The
Ten Commandments

The Ten Commandments

From the Shadow of Eden To the Promise of Canaan

by

Dennis S. Ross

BIBAL Press
North Richland Hills, Texas

BIBAL Press
An imprint of D. & F. Scott Publishing, Inc.
P.O. Box 821653
N. Richland Hills, TX 76182
info@dfscott.com
www.dfscott.com
1-888-788-2280

Copyright © 2000 by Dennis S. Ross

All rights reserved. No part of this book may be reproduced in any manner whatsoever without written permission of the publisher except for brief quotations embodied in critical articles or reviews.

Printed in the United States of America

04 03 02 01 00   5 4 3 2 1

Library of Congress Cataloging-in-Publication Data
Ross, Dennis S. (Dennis Sidney), 1953-
 From the shadow of Eden to the promise of Canaan / by Dennis S. Ross.
  p. cm.
 ISBN 1-930566-01-8 (alk. paper)
 1. Ten commandments—Criticism, interpretation, etc., Jewish. 2. Sabbath. I. Title.
BM520.75 .R67 2000
296.3'6—dc21
                                00-010972

Cover image by Rebecca Aaron
Cover photography by Michael D'Amore, Sunshine Photographics, Pittsfield, Massachusetts
All other images copyright ©2000 by ww.arttoday.com

To Debbie:
Everything is possible with you.

Contents

Preface		ix
Introduction		xi
1	The Ten Commandments on CD-ROM: A Scene Moses Never Imagined	1
2	Thought: Coveting the Mechanical Ox	13
3	Speech: What Do You Say to an Anxious Bride?	27
4	Family, Parents, and Spouse: The Human Stepstool	35
5	Community: A History of Strangers and the Responsibility of Redeemers	45
6	God: The Cosmic 800 Number and Divine Next Day Mail	59
7	God's Sabbath: The Existential Epic: More Than Just a Day of Rest	69
8	The Sabbath: Time and Space	85
9	God's Sabbath: Having and Being	95
10	God's Sabbath: Ends and Means	103

Preface

This book is a product of Torah study—Bible classes that wrestle with the ideas expressed by the sacred text and its rabbinic interpreters. I thank my students, both adults and children, in the congregations I have served as rabbi: Temple Beth El of Northern Westchester in Chappaqua, New York; Washington Hebrew Congregation in Washington, DC; and, most of all in these last eight years, the deeply caring members of Temple Anshe Amunim in Pittsfield, Massachusetts.

Rabbi Chaim Stern and Rabbi Jack Stern put forward many significant suggestions. Marc Jaffe was most helpful at all levels, from concept to finish. Rabbi William Cutter, Rabbi A. Stanley Dreyfus, Dr. Philip Miller, Rabbi H. Leonard Poller, Rabbi Harold Salzmann, and Albert Vorspan provided valuable support. Louise Stern made editorial contributions. Rebecca Aaron and Marjorie Reder offered editorial assistance. All translations from Hebrew are my own.

Our children, Joshua, Adam, and Miriam, bless me with their curiosity. My wife, Rabbi Deborah Zecher, always encourages my writing. I dedicate this book to her.

Rabbi Dennis S. Ross
Pittsfield, Massachusetts
September 11, 2000
Elul 11, 5760

Moses Holding the Tablets of the Covenant
(painting by J. James Tissot)

Introduction

Two oval-topped tablets, standing side by side—everyone recognizes the religious symbol. But get to specifics—"You shall" and "You shall not"—it seems there is not much recognition at all. When a recent public opinion survey inquired, "Have you heard of the Ten Commandments," the answer was "Yes, of course!" But when asked to name all Ten Commandments, the typical participant could not come up with more than a couple. And when the surveyors described the overlooked commandments, participants were not happy with what they heard.

The Ten Commandments, more than just a "prep book" for taking opinion polls, presents the Ten Commandments as understood by Judaism, the religion of the people who gave the Ten Commandments to the world. Jewish sages, known as rabbis, interpreted and taught the Bible over the centuries. One little-known sage, Abraham bar Hiyya of eleventh-century Spain, took a unique approach to the Ten Commandments, organizing the precepts by meaning instead of number, by categories of thought, speech, and action, in relation to family, community, and God. One thousand years ago, Rabbi Abraham used the Ten Commandments to weave a sense of spirituality through community, describing God in relationships with other people. And his nuanced, practical religious vision inspires and enables today.

The Ten Commandments were written three thousand years ago in a part of the world called the Ancient Near East. Long ago in that region, each nation put forward its own list of rules, law codes that all grew outmoded and disappeared. Chapter 1 of *The Ten Commandments* describes why the Ten Commandments, instead of becoming extinct, are still around—and thriving. And Rabbi Abraham bar Hiyya shows how the Decalogue and its associated teachings turn the "Shadow of Eden into the Promise of Canaan."

Commandments of thought, the First Commandment (faith in God) and the Tenth Commandment (prohibiting "coveting"), are the focus of chapter 2. The Ten Commandments strive for a consistency of thinking and doing, how thought and action can be one.

Often, it is simple to speak the truth; sometimes it is difficult. In chapter 3, Commandments Three and Nine of speech (speech about God and speech in court, respectively) examine the spoken word in relation to community and God.

Commandments Five and Seven concern the family—parents and spouse. In chapter 4, thought and speech, leading to actions toward immediate relatives, carry the essence of the outward reaching, "other-directed" spirituality of the Jewish tradition.

Every community views the world through the perspective of its history. In chapter 5, memory of the Jewish slave experience grows into the responsibility to help free others who are also oppressed. For instance, in Commandment Four about Sabbath, all classes of a society, powerful and weak, rich and poor, are granted a rest day under the protection of the Covenant between God and the people of Israel. How well a society cares for the

INTRODUCTION

powerless—the rights that the stranger enjoys—is the standard for judging the goodness of that society.

The Second Commandment prohibits idolatry (what idolatry was and what it means today is a topic for chapter 9). In considering the response to idolatry, chapter 6 introduces the theology of *The Ten Commandments*, raising ideas about God and the ideal life, concepts at the center of the book's later chapters. In response to religious traditions that often see God as a source of retribution, chapter 6 takes a serious look at questions about "theodicy," God's justice.

Commandment Four, of the Sabbath, is the capstone of the creation story and the entire Decalogue. Yes, the Sabbath is a day to follow God's example and refrain from work. Chapter 7 presents the Sabbath as a way to escape from the shadow of the curse of Eden and bring about the promise of Canaan, healing the world of hardship and suffering.

Chapter 8 describes the achievable spiritual goal of the Sabbath. In a workweek society that attends to sacred *space*, the Sabbath establishes sacred *time*. This chapter is based upon a wonderful little book, *The Sabbath* by Rabbi Abraham Joshua Heschel, and shows how time offers a special spiritual opportunity.

Erich Fromm, in *To Have or to Be?*, redefines idolatry as an emphasis of *having* over *being*. Chapter 9 explores the workweek tension between economics and relationships and presents the Sabbath as an opportunity to reconcile the tension between what we own and what we are.

Finally, chapter 10 summarizes and establishes the Sabbath blueprint—the Decalogue's utopian vision. This world labors under the "Shadow of Eden." With the "promise of Canaan," time and space, having and being, ends and means all come under bar Hiyya's ideal of family, community, and God.

THE TEN COMMANDMENTS

The world *has* changed in the three thousand years since the Ten Commandments came to the fore. Yet there is something wonderful and strong about the Ten Commandments that endures. The Decalogue is not list of deadly sins, but a living tradition. In an era of unclear and conflicting spiritual messages, the Ten Commandments integrate a foundation of civilization into modern life, setting forward ideals to live with and goals to live for. Modern times often see the paradox of material fullness hand in hand with spiritual uncertainty—people seem unhappy, even though it appears that they have everything. Too often, professional achievement, economic prosperity, and social acclaim stand side by side with inner questioning about the purpose and direction of life. So the Ten Commandments can help today. First, it is important to see what they achieved thirty centuries ago, what made this law code different than others back then, and why it endures. Then and only then will we see what it tells us for today.

The Ten Commandments on CD-ROM
A Scene Moses Never Imagined

At a local college library, I headed for a computer terminal, and typed in "Ten Commandments." As the CD-ROM raced through *The Readers' Guide to Periodical Literature*, I searched my memory. In the pre-computer era of my student days, as a sort of library slave, I turned by hand hundreds of pages in those heavy red volumes indexing popular publications. Then the computer screen announced its revelation: nearly two hundred listings.

"What a find!" I gasped, like a scholar of sacred - literature unearthing a cache of long lost ancient manuscripts. Then, one-by-one, the computer quickly and mindlessly coughed up references ranging from "Ten Commandments of Maternity Wear," and "Ten Commandments for Stretching for Running" to the "Ten Commandments for Safe Meat Handling," "Ten Commandments for Successful Baseball Stadium Construction" and finally a magazine cartoon of a man shoplifting "The Ten Commandments" video.

"This is a joke!" I muttered. "I wanted theology, not comedy!"

But, in the car on the way home, I realized that the very information that at first seemed silly and irrelevant had, in fact, accidentally yielded conclusive proof. The computer, distant descendent of ancient parchment, had documented that the format of Ten Commandments is indelibly ingrained in contemporary life. In the three millennia since the Decalogue was put forth, no one has said it any better: "If you want people's attention, do it in ten.

We have tens and tens of "decalogues," from the "List of the Ten Most Actively Traded" of the New York Stock Exchange to the "Top Ten" hitters in major league baseball. Well past the nation's bedtime, entertainer David Letterman props open millions of drowsy eyes with his humorous tallies of ten. *Aseret Hadibrot*, as they are called in Hebrew, literally "ten words," teach all of us—entertainers, economists, professional athletes, and clergy—if it's important, say it in ten.

With a Bible on almost every home bookshelf and a list of ten on almost everyone's lips, it is hard to imagine the need for another book about the Ten Commandments. *From the Shadow of Eden to the Promise of Canaan* began forty years ago when Rabbi Bernstein placed the sweetness of the "Kawmetz alef, aw, kawmetz beis baw" of the Torah's Hebrew language on my tongue. In seminary, after my secular college education, I took a more substantial taste of two thousand years of rabbinic comprehension and interpretation of sacred text. There, I gained a richer appreciation of the classic rabbis, who gave Torah the scrutiny of a skeptical jeweler carefully studying a gem under an eye loupe. Much has been said about the Ten Commandments, (too much, in fact—important concepts have been buried among the too many words, largely unnoticed for centuries).

I eventually figured out how to get what I needed from the library computer—the latest word on these eternal "ten words," what they say and what they mean, what made them the center of Jewish religious life and the bedrock of Western civilization. In my research, I discovered the stunning eleventh-century writings of Rabbi Abraham bar Hiyya of Barcelona, Spain. Bar Hiyya brilliantly presented the Ten Commandments in a conceptual order rather than a number order; he grouped the laws of the Decalogue by idea instead of by numerical sequence. But before considering bar Hiyya's innovative approach, we need to consider a little ancient history.

It seems everyone today has a list, and it was the same in Bible times. Like Israel, most nations across the Ancient Near East had their own law codes that sometimes looked like the Ten Commandments. For instance, modern Bible scholar Nahum Sarna points to the writings of historians and archaeologists (*Exploring Exodus*, Schocken, 1986, p. 132 ff.) who carefully reviewed the official documents of the peoples of the Ancient Near East. Sarna tells us of the Hittites (of 1400 to 1200 BCE, just prior to Israel's exodus from Egypt), a nation of military conquerors who forcibly occupied parts of the lands that we today call Turkey and Syria, and then imposed treaties on the peoples they overran. These treaties, on the surface, resembled the Ten Commandments. The treaties generally contained:

- A *preamble*, or opening statement, describing the Hittite leader writing the agreement.
- A *historical review* summarizing what happened to make a treaty necessary. Together, the preamble and the historical review established the author's authority and the treaty's legitimacy.
- At the heart of the treaty were *stipulations*, a detailed list of the treaty's directives.
- The *deposition*, instructions for the storage of the sacred documents and for their public reading.

- A list of *witnesses*.
- A description of *curses and blessings*, consequences of obedience or violation of the treaty's rules—what happened to those who listened and disobeyed.

Like a Hittite treaty, the Ten Commandments begin with a summary of the recently shared experiences of the major figures, God and Israel.

In the *preamble* and *historic review*, the Ten Commandments open with the statement:

> *I, the Eternal, am your God who brought you out of the land of Egypt, the house of bondage.*

There follows a statement that identifies the Decalogue's initiator—the mighty and benevolent God—and reminds the people of Israel of what had just happened—the wonder-filled exodus from Egypt at the hand of that God.

From that exodus to the challenges of wandering through the Sinai Desert, from the ten plagues God inflicted on the Egyptians to the parting of the Sea of Reeds, ancient Israel benefited from God's generosity without having to do anything in return. God gave and Israel took. Now the Ten Commandments open a new chapter in the relationship between God and Israel.

The *preamble* and *historic review* of the Ten Commandments mark that turning point; the once one-sided relationship now becomes mutual. The remaining nine of the Ten Commandments—and a good portion of the rest of the Five Books of Moses—outline the *stipulations*, the details of Israel's reciprocal responsibilities to God. The prohibitions of idolatry, the false oath, murder, adultery, stealing, bearing false witness, and coveting, the injunctions to observe the Sabbath, honor parents, and more, all fall on Israel, as a "national debt" so to speak—what Israel owes God for the redemption. Israel now repays a spiritual obligation not in dollars, but through behavior, by living the way God wants life to be lived—by following a code of precepts that have come to be called the Ten Commandments.

According to the *deposition*, the tablets of the Commandments were stored in the Ark of the Covenant (Exod 25:16). The Bible elsewhere speaks of heaven and earth as the *witnesses*, as well as blessings and curses, rewards for keeping the law, the *blessings* of national well-being—prosperity, fertile harvests, good health, protection from enemies, peace—and harsh consequences of breaking the law—*curses* that include poverty, famine, plague, and war (Leviticus 26).

Thus, when it comes to structure and organization, the Hittite treaty and the Ten Commandments appear to us as textual cousins. Both present their material in a similar way. Some scholars believe this parallel is merely an interesting coincidence, dumb luck without theological, cultural, or religious significance. Others suggest that one nation took the idea from the other, as if some linen or perfume caravan driver bartered off a "boilerplate" text of a law code—or even the germ of an idea—leaving it to the local religious and political authorities to "fill in" the historical and legal details. Some call the Bible's version the official "Word of God" as transcribed by Moses, and the Hittite text a "cheap imitation" of the real thing. But I am convinced that a debate over the origins of the Ten Commandments misses *the* important point. It makes little difference if or how an ancient international traveling salesperson hawked a load of spices and an imaginative list of regulations. There is a remarkable *superficial* resemblance between the Hittite treaty and the Decalogue, but these similarities are unimportant. Before we jump to the conclusion that the Hittite and Israelite legal codes are cut from the same cloth—or carved out of pieces of the same stone—we look a little more carefully into the content. The crucial differences become very clear.

Difference Number 1: National Continuity

Consider not a difference about the laws, but a difference about the people who wrote and tried to implement the laws. Historians tell us that many societies populated the Ancient Near East across Egypt, Palestine, Lebanon, Turkey, and Mesopotamia. The Bible talks of various peoples such as the Perrizites, Girgashites, Amalekites, Canaanites, and more. They and the mighty Hittite conquerors vanished into history. Their cultures, languages, and religions are extinct. The nation Israel, on the other hand, is still here, alive and flourishing. The first difference, then, is Israel's *continuity*. Israel and its Decalogue are today alive, whereas they and theirs are not. And why is this small player, Israel, still on the field long after the others are gone? Let us pursue the answer.

Difference Number 2: Equality

Among the Hittites and others of Bible times, there was one set of rules for the powerless poor and one set for the powerful wealthy. In the typical law book of the ancient Near East, when a pauper knocked out the tooth of a noble, the injury could cost the pauper's life. But, when a noble did the same to a pauper, the rules usually called for nothing more than a small fine against the noble. All across the Ancient Near East, the powerful and the mighty wrote laws to benefit and protect themselves at the expense of the local underlings. But among the followers of Moses, for the first time ever, all were treated equally under the law. The second difference: the Ten Commandments are universal, applying to everyone *equally* and to the entire community collectively. For example, the Fifth Commandment, the flat-out insistence to honor parents is incumbent on an entire population, the rich and the impoverished, the homeborn and the stranger under all circumstances.

Difference Number 3: Eternality

Typically in the Ancient Near East, the decrees of the Girgashites, the Hittite, and the others lasted only as long as the rulers that wrote them. But in Israel, the Ten Commandments always held force, regardless of who was in power. "You shall not steal" means "Do not take anything from anyone, ever."

The Bible's Ten Commandments are not a daily tally of regulations most frequently broken or a moving index of precepts most widely observed. Whether we find it in a computer, a book, handwritten on parchment or etched into the face of a rock, the Decalogue is not a product of a market study, or like the Hittite treaty, a child of political expediency. With all today's popularity lists, the items change so often they might as well be written in erasable ink. The Hittites only hint at it, but the Ten Commandments and much of the Bible are founded on it. Universally and eternally binding, the Ten Commandments, the Bible's distillation and expression of everlasting truth, carved into stone some three thousand years ago, are as close to the philosopher's "categorical imperative" as you can get. Difference three: The Ten Commandments stand *eternal* and unchanging, forever.

Difference Number 4: Theology

Where other treaties come from mortal monarchs, the Decalogue tells us it comes from God. And this theological document transforms a bunch of ragtag former slaves, broken-spirited and of shattered soul, into an entirely new and exalted "nation of priests," living in direct relationship with that God. Where the Hittite international treaties were political, economic, and social documents defining the relationship between a human ruler and human citizens, the Ten Commandments are a Covenant, a spiritual pact between God and Israel.

Yes, the Ten Commandments are a tool of governing, serving the political purpose of transforming a disorganized group of slaves into a sophisticated nation. But first and foremost, the Ten Commandments are a *theological* and ethical contract, a religious pact between a nation and its God, simultaneously safeguarding and extending the spiritual dignity of God *and* Israel. And as we consider one more theological aspect of the Decalogue, we will see how the Ten Commandments speak to us today with as much substance and force as ever.

Now the doubt-filled reader, having gotten this far, may respond to my words with the following argument: "After three millennia of striving to be honest in court, laying off idols and offering homage to our God, establishing Medicare to honor our parents, dispensing justice to our murderers and robbers, we have done a fairly decent job meeting our obligation to God. We paid our debt for the exodus. After all, religion only divides people. Isn't there enough fragmentation in our world? Why have any religion at all? We need to bring people together as one peacefully, united humanity. Enough already with this covenant!"

If this is your argument or if you want to make one that resembles it, I ask you to read on because the Bible and the Ten Commandments offer humanity a one-of-a-kind message, a unique assessment of our collective spiritual condition, and a prescription for improving it.

From the Shadow of Eden To the Promise of Canaan

The Torah (the Five books of Moses, or the Pentateuch, the first five books of the Bible) that is home to the Ten Commandments, opens with a stunning description of God's creation—of the sun, moon, and earth; water and dry land; vegetation, animal, and human life. One might have expected the biblical creation narrative to achieve a breathtaking climactic conclusion, with the first man and woman lovingly holding hands in Eden's panorama under the warming sunlight of God's newly fashioned heavens. But this majestic creation tale, with all its power and its dignity, culminates in an *un*happy ending. The lesson of the Genesis story is not bliss but a curse: Adam and Eve disobey God and eat Eden's forbidden fruit. In punishment for the first couple's first transgression, God banishes Adam and Eve from paradise, damns the earth that gave them life and has now become their final destination. God further curses the relationships between Eve and Adam and between Eve and her child. And as death enters the world, the curse of Eden becomes the tragic metaphor for the despair and misery that we might call the human condition.

See how the Bible develops the "epic theme" of the cursed earth. Cain bloodies the ground with the life of his brother, Abel. In Noah's time, continuing collective misdeeds turn the entire land "corrupt." In Babel, people try to flee from the land by building an edifice skyward. In the following chapters, the patriarchs and matriarchs, a family of wandering nomads, traverse the Ancient Near East, calling no site on this earth "home." And the damnation culminates in Egypt, where Pharaoh shackles the people of Israel to the cursed earth in rigorous slavery and fulfills Eve's curse by murdering the women's offspring at birth. Chapter by chapter, the curse deepens and darkens. The bondage to the earth intensifies until two small but pivotal stories begin the transformation from curse to blessing, from death to life. In two narratives of the women of Israel, one, a warm-spirited tale of a pair of resourceful midwives and, the other, a dramatic plot of a mother and a sister saving a baby, the Torah offers the transitional vignettes of the epic. The women begin to break the curse and direct the nation toward redemption. God frees the people from Egypt to the promise of the land Canaan. Once cursed like all other lands, Canaan now flows with milk and honey instead of the thorns and grasses it sprouted in previous days. And here we have the thesis of the book: the Ten Commandments, and their associated laws and rituals, set the paradigm for the cursed earth to flower and blossom. The Ten Commandments transform a lonely, embarrassed, and terrified first couple into God's people living on a promised land. The Ten Commandments are the tools for overcoming the fundamental problems of human existence, and for forging a social, political, economic, ecological, and theological harmony. The covenant of the Ten Commandments can remove Eden's curse, restore the land's fertility, renew the love of the estranged husband and wife, and make the miracle of birth a blessing. Through the Ten Commandments, all of society, each woman and man is restored and approaches the harmony that once was Eden's.

Seven weeks after God saved the people of Israel from Pharaoh, the Ten Commandments belonged to Israel. Inside the Ark of the Covenant, a wooden container overlaid with hand-beaten gold, the people stored our Decalogue's tablets. For the next forty years, an entire nation trudged across the Sinai wilderness, the sun and great weight of our sacred cargo of wood and metal on our shoulders. Israel bore that burden for four decades because of the profound significance of the "Ten Words" inside that box, the blueprint for redeeming ourselves.

A rarely quoted Jewish scholar, Abraham bar Hiyya of eleventh-century Barcelona, Spain, left us the key to that golden container. Writing in Hebrew for the educated Jewish reader, bar Hiyya was a philosopher, mathematician, astronomer, and translator. One of his many works, *Hegyon Hanefesh Heatsuvah*—in English, *Meditation on the Sad Soul*—offers an ingenious framework for interpreting the Ten Commandments. According to bar Hiyya, the Ten Commandments contain a glimmer of all the Torah's commandments; there is a conceptual connection between the Ten Commandments and each one of the Torah's remaining 603 commandments. And when we follow the Ten Commandments, according to bar Hiyya, by honoring our universal and eternal Covenant, we imitate God, the Creator and Redeemer, and turn the curse of Eden into the blessing of Canaan and liberate ourselves from the heartaches of the human condition.

In bar Hiyya's footsteps, my work opens with the most basic unit of society, the individual, his or her thoughts, speech, and actions. I then turn to the family, to the community and then to God, going from the smallest sphere of activity of the individual, to the greatest sphere, God, whose all-encompassing covenant with Israel culminates in the Sabbath and its prescription for the life of harmony. Through the concepts underlying the Sabbatical and Jubilee, the Decalogue promises us that people, animal life, and the entire earth will all become ends in themselves and not means to the goal of someone or something else. In short, through our Ten Commandments we overturn a curse and discover blessing, and transform Eden's shadow into Canaan's promise.

Thought
Coveting the Mechanical Ox

Rabbi Abraham bar Hiyya would have us begin with commandments of thought. Two commandments—the First Commandment and the Tenth Commandment—illustrate. But first, let's read two stories.

Each day of the workweek, in a spontaneous motorized collaboration, truck drivers in a rush to deliver things, sanitation workers in no hurry to haul other things away, joined double-parked automobile commuters to block the major traffic arteries and minor side-street capillaries of New York, the city of my birth. Not towing, not high fines, not high fines combined with towing fees that exceeded the value of the more traffic weary impounded cars could deter drivers from ignoring the ubiquitous "No Parking, Tow Away Zone" signs. Then the Mayor had an idea. On street poles across the city suddenly appeared new, even more forthright and forceful signs reading, "Don't even THINK of parking here!" as if to say, "Move your thoughts and your vehicle to a different place."

I think I remember something of the typical raucous New York controversy that followed the Mayor's innovation. A few seasoned political observers praised the Mayor's ingenuity, while others, as could be expected, denounced it. Some spoke against the new

13

signs as "public relations gimmickry" instead of the "sound urban planning" that was urgently needed. "Finally," declared some others in exasperation, "The Mayor is concerned with what the citizens of this city really think." And still others could have offered the following imaginary newspaper headline: "New Crime Wave Strikes City: Thinking!" subtitled, "The Mayor's Dictatorial Efforts to Impose Thought Control."

Not long ago I was speaking to an Elderhostel class about the commandments of thought and the Mayor's new sign. A hand went into the air.

"Rabbi, do you remember the Broadway musical, *The Most Happy Fella?*

"Sure, it's one of my favorites."

"So do you remember the lyrics of the song, 'Standing on the Corner Watching All the Girls Go By?' Well, do you remember the verse that went like this?" And he started to sing, in a clear but wobbly voice, "Brother, you can't go to jail for what you're thinking."

Then he continued speaking. "Well, Rabbi, what would your Mayor think of that? If you listen to the Mayor, literally, it's a crime to think, but if you listen to Lerner and Lowe, they can't put you behind bars for it!"

And that, in a playful way of asking, is just the question. What is the crime in what you think?

The self—its thought, its speech, and its action—in relation to family, community and God, leads us to begin with two commandments, the first and the last, both commandments of thought, commandments of the mind. We can approach this commandment of "thought control" by beginning with the Tenth and final Commandment.

> *You shall not covet your neighbor's house. You shall not covet your neighbor's spouse, male or female servants, ox, donkey or anything that is your neighbor's.*

THOUGHT

Another "Don't even THINK"—this one from Scripture, telling us to turn our thoughts away from wanting what belongs to another. City Hall critics can afford to poke fun at a flamboyant mayor and the tongue-in-cheek demand that city residents control what they think. But there is little of that sense of satire in a Bible that takes this issue very seriously. So let us leave the former Mayor to himself and ask a few questions of our Torah.

In a world where "You can't go to jail for what you're thinking," the mind has a mind of its own. "Our thoughts are beyond our control," people say. "Our thoughts are destined to run free. We cannot turn on commendable ideas or turn off bad ones the way we flip the switch on the family room light. How could a God of justice and fairness punish us for something we cannot stop doing? A compassionate God, One who understands how we are made, One quick to forgive our failings, should certainly recognize the longing gaze I cast at the empty space in front of the fire hydrant." Let us turn to the words of the rabbis, the sages of the sacred text and the eye loupes.

Our classic teachers thought, talked, and wrote from the beginning of the Common Era until just shortly before modern times. Textual experts, they lived in Israel, Egypt, and what we today know as Iran, Iraq, and Yemen. Their writings, the Midrash and the Talmud interpret the Bible's text for us, offering explanations that address the big picture and the detail as well. And we will get to know these rabbis in the pages ahead. But first, another story.

When my family and I moved to the Berkshires several years ago, our first major mountain winter storm left twelve inches of wet, heavy snow on our twenty-foot long, double-car width driveway. When we had lived outside Washington, DC, a winter earlier, I hand shoveled away in twenty minutes a typical two-inch snow covering. In the Berkshires, a foot of slush is typical, and, left untouched, by nightfall freezes into a rock-solid, icy moonscape, rendering a driveway impassable until a major thaw months afterward. Here in Western Massachusetts, shoveling snow is a major excavation.

To avoid back strain, I lopped off only little chunks as if I were cutting into a party cake, keeping pieces small to make sure there would be enough to serve all the guests. I worked up a sweat, took off my coat, then my hat, then my sweater—and after three-quarters of an hour I was only half done. Holding the shovel level to keep the heavy, damp snow from sliding off began to feel like balancing a load of wet newspapers on the end of a broomstick. I stopped to rest and to study my achievements—a square of clear asphalt and a growing pile of slush that, by tomorrow morning, would freeze into an abstract ice sculpture.

Then I noticed a neighbor across the street. In a moment, he emerged from his garage, driving a gas-powered snowthrower that filled the neighborhood with noise and the air with a tail of smoke—and then a blast of snow. He cleared a twenty-foot swath in no time. As I went back to work I imagined the city snow plow coming by while I slept, pushing up a snow-turned-to-ice wall at the driveway's end which, when I left for work next morning, would rip my car's exhaust system from its under-vehicle moorings. Just then, I WANTED A SNOWBLOWER. I coveted that thousand-dollar mechanical ox, that high-priced, gas-powered beast of burden. Now here is my question: Did I violate the Ten Commandments?

The rabbis do not view the world in black and white or even in shades of gray—they always seem to add a little red and blue as if only to complicate the situation. In other words, there is a big disappointment ahead for those who expect the rabbis will answer "Yes" or "No" or give it to us in a single sentence. We can group their responses in four broad categories:

1) **The Passing Desire.** Very few of the rabbis haVE a problem with my momentary longing for a snowblower, or, for that matter, a city driver's passing reverie about an illegal parking space or a country boy's hankering for a neighbor's field. It may come as a surprise, but to the majority of those who think and write in the Jewish tradition, there is no sin in the passing thought, sinful as the thought may be. "Don't even THINK?" Not really. You can't be jailed if that is all you do.

2) **A Lusting of the Heart.** What about a deeper longing? To a handful of the sages, the sin is lusting for a particular item. The minute my longing to own "an ox" becomes a longing for "that ox across the street that will get my job done so much faster, the one that is not for sale," I have sinned. "Don't even THINK?" While most rabbis find nothing wrong in lusting for a particular "one," to some rabbis, you can think all you want—until you start thinking about "that one."

3) **Formulating a Plan.** Regarding anything else on or off the Torah's list, you can want something; you can even want a specific something or someone very badly. To a few more of the sages, the sin comes only when we concoct a scheme, when we develop a plan for securing what is not rightfully ours. So when we convince ourselves that the grass may be greener on the neighbor's side of the fence, or the neighbor's ox is a little stronger, we commit no sin. "Don't even think?" To an added handful of the rabbis, think all you want, but don't develop a specific strategy.

4) **Acting on a Desire.** There is nothing wrong in longing for an object, or for a specific object, say most of the rabbis. And there is nothing wrong in formulating a plan to get hold of it. The majority opinion is this—the sin is in acting to get it. "Don't even think?"

> These are all sins of the mind and, the rabbis say, they are of no consequence. Only when there is an action is there a sin.

Yes, it is a pragmatic, realistic approach, to teach that "You can't go to jail for what you're thinking." What you *do* is all that counts. But before we conclude that we have a "no sweat" covenant, that "Hizzonor," the Mayor, was wrong, that the guys standing on the corner had it right, that thoughts do not count at all, that you can think all you want and the promised land will be within quick reach so we can hurry off to the next chapter, let us first turn to another commandment of thought, that is, the First Commandment.

> *I am the Eternal, your God, who brought you out of the land of Egypt, from a house of bondage.*

This is a commandment? It looks like a statement of history that reminds us who took us from where, that God redeemed us from Egypt. As a commandment, it does not seem to be asking much of us.

As we saw in the opening chapter, the "scientific" consensus says that the First Commandment, like a Hittite preamble, briefly recapitulates Israel's most recent history. It commands nothing, but, as a literary device, quickly summarizes what just happened. It is the Bible's way of saying, "Now you owe me." To the scientist, then, the Ten Commandments open, not with a commandment, but with a statement, one sentence about the "who" and the "what" of the history of the exodus.

"Don't even THINK of the Ten Commandments that way!" the classic rabbis volley back in our first encounter with the feud between the contemporary scientist/biblical literary analyst and the traditional theologian. Yes, our classical rabbis, by and large from medieval times, retort with, "It is not a preamble, but a commandment. It is not an appetizer; it is the main course. It is not some Jewish takeoff on an ancient Hittite treaty. The First Commandment comes from the Torah. It is a divine work, not a product of the human hand. And as Sacred Literature, Torah is studied and understood according to the rules of hermeneutics, rules of religious interpretation. To treat the Bible like the literature of Shakespeare or the Iliad, to study the Bible as if it were a historical document such as the Declaration of Independence or the Magna Carta, is to dance with blasphemy. Each one of the Ten Commandments is the word of God. Each one, the first included, insists that we do something!"

So who is right, the rabbis or the scientists? Let us take the next step. Dear rabbis, if one believes that

> *I am the Eternal, your God, who brought you out of the land of Egypt, from a house of bondage*

is a commandment, then tell us, please, what this commandment is commanding? After all, other commandments offer a clear impression of what is expected. "You shall not steal" means, "Don't take anything that does not belong to you." And "Remember the Sabbath day" wants us to rest one day in seven. But what does "I brought you out of the land of Egypt, the house of bondage" want you and me to do?

Again our sages diverge in their thinking. To most rabbis, we have in this introductory commandment an overall demand of loyalty, requiring a pledge of allegiance to God. It is the Bible's way of saying, when it comes to looking elsewhere for the truth, "Don't even THINK!" But when we ask, "How shall we think? What shall we believe?" we again stumble into disagreement. Again, centuries of religious interpretation of the sacred text show a clear disunity of approach to this verse; the rabbis break into two camps the rational-oriented rabbis, on the one hand, and on the other, those who emphasize faith.

The *rationalists*, in the tradition of Maimonides, tell us that this is a cognitive commandment, a commandment for the religious mind. To the rationalists, this First Commandment describes our God as the "Prime Cause" in the universe, the source of all truth, knowledge, being and life. Just as we know that law of nature that tells us the white stuff on my driveway boils at 212 degrees Fahrenheit and freezes at 32 Fahrenheit, we should know, cognitively, that God made the world and God took us out of Egypt, just as the Bible says. It is a statement of fact. A cognitive understanding of "I, the Eternal . . ." means we should know that the Ten Commandments—and the universe—start with God of the Creation and the Redemption.

Where the rational interpretation appeals to the *mind*, the second interpretation, of *faith*, speaks to the *heart*.

I am the Eternal, your God, who brought you out of the land of Egypt, the house of bondage

is a commandment, not of the head, but of the spirit. The rationalists say we prove there is a God the way we prove water boils or freezes. To the faithful, God will be there the way drinkable water will flow when I turn on the faucet, hot with this handle, cold with the other. Faith is different from belief. Faith is conjecture, hope, wishing and longing—but not fact. Rational belief in God means *knowing* God; faith is *trust*, a confidence in God.

Either way, for the classic rabbinic rationalists and for the classic rabbinic faithful, "I am the Eternal, your God" is an internal, personal, almost invisible commandment of the self, a commandment of thought, a commandment about all God's commandments.

You might claim that my colleagues, past and present, join me in making too much of the details.

THOUGHT

Why nit-pick? Just say it, straight and simple, and leave the rest as it is. Why not just say that belief in God, trust in God, are the essential covenantal obligations, fundamental Jewish religious duties? And just as there ought to be an enforceable law against illegal parking, there ought to be a law against theological double-talk. Religious nuance? "Don't even think of it!"

But how do we answer the imaginary critics of the Mayor? What will the Mayor do when the chorus of "The Most Happy Fella" bounds out of their Broadway theater chanting "You can't go to jail for what you're thinking," to lure theatergoers to consider leaving the car right under the sparkling new "Don't even THINK" sign? How do you command people *not* to think, be it a thought of parking, a fleeting longing for a sexual encounter, or even a forbidden thought of an alien divinity?

It seems to me that we cannot command thought, belief, or faith. After all, the mind seems to have a mind of its own. How do we cultivate a particular thought in the mind and how do we make blossom a special feeling in the heart? How do we enforce a faith or demand a belief, regulate trust, or legislate understanding? And what about the times we have legitimate questions of faith? Is not ours a religious tradition that encourages us to struggle with doubt and wrestle with the angel of uncertainty? And if people do violate this contemplative commandment, how do we put the mind or the heart on the witness stand? If people speak against God, it is blasphemy, a sin of speech, not a sin of thought, and that belongs in the next chapter. If people pray to another God, their active participation in the ritual of a foreign faith can be proven. But even then, so what? Are we going to begin an inquisition? After all, we are who we are and we will think and feel what we want—and this is one awful way to begin our discussion of the sacred Ten Commandments, with confusion! To think that we face the possibility of eight more chapters of this agitated argumentation! But the situation is not that bleak.

Personally, I believe this First Commandment is a preamble. Yes, it is a historic summary. But when we come to the rabbis, I have to take pause. Yes, the classic rabbinic interpretations of the First Commandment fall into dichotomies, this *or* that, yes *or* no, history *or* theology, faith *or* belief. And yes, the classic rabbinic interpretation of the Tenth Commandment falls into a hierarchy, from less to more, a progression of wanting one, wanting a particular one, planning to get that one, and acting on that longing. And this grid of "yes or no" and "less to more," "black" to "white" and "darkening shades of gray" offers two different approaches to the world. Together, they tell us that what we think is very important to the Torah.

Some fifteen years ago, a call for a funeral led to my meeting with the deceased man's daughter and son-in-law before the funeral ceremony.

"There is not much good you can say about my Dad, Rabbi," sighed the daughter. "He was a sour, angry man. There is nothing good to say."

The Ten Commandments flashed before my eyes—honoring parents, family, telling the truth, honesty. I gulped as I saw myself standing there in the funeral chapel, in front of dozens of relatives and friends, with nothing at all to say. Then I had an idea. I asked a question.

"What made him that way?"

"To tell you the truth, Rabbi, he did a lot of dreaming, and none of his dreams for himself came true. He wanted to become an accountant; he wound up going to war. He wanted to go to college after the war; he had to go into the family business. He wanted to work with his mind; instead, he had to work with his hands. He was angry and frustrated his whole life."

I never got past their first sentence. "He dreamed. In other words, he was a man who dreamed."

"Well, yes, Rabbi. You could say that. And you know, we made his dreams come true for him. I went to school to become a lawyer. My husband is a doctor. And my brother went to school to become an accountant. And he was very proud of our achievements. He acted as if they were his and they were."

Not only did I have what to say, the daughter and son-in-law now saw him in a different, better way. No longer was he some frustrated and angry failure. Now he was a proud father. One question and their attitude shifted 180 degrees.

The *consistency* of thought, speech, and deed is the focus of our Covenant. Sometimes, attaining that consistency means we have to change what we think, so that we take on a positive attitude. "Don't even THINK of your father like that. Let's try to think of him in a different way. No, you can't go to jail for having those thoughts. But if you remember only the bitter, negative experiences, you will imprison yourself whenever you think of him. By thinking of the cup half full instead of half empty we honor the commandment of thought."

The commandment of thought describes the attitudes we take, how we understand, interpret, and explain what happens to us, and instructs us to take a positive approach to life. When the First Commandment recalls we were in "the house of bondage," it does not look to place blame or insist we return to that land of Egypt to even up the score. The First Commandment sets an optimistic tone for the following nine. We do not ruminate over the bitter but, as we will see in coming chapters, to have faith/belief in God is to strive to find a positive approach and look ahead with hope. This is the religious meaning of the commandment to think.

"Don't even THINK of parking here!" was a *rhetorical* statement. Even the Mayor would admit that no one should have to go to jail for a feeling, pay a fine for an impulse, or suffer any punishment for the careful consideration of leaving a car in an illegal space. "Don't even think" and "You shall not covet" are examples of common speech that communicate, "What we think is a serious matter because thought impacts life." In fact, we can put ourselves into a jail of sorts for what we are thinking, when an obsession for power, financial success, or prestige keeps us from seeing and living. When we concentrate too many of life's efforts in one direction, when we sacrifice all for the sake of a little, we lose perspective and ignore what is really important—our purpose for being on this earth, why we are here and what we are supposed to accomplish. I will speak more about this later, when we come to turning a cursed earth into a promised land.

In sum, Commandments One and Ten together want us to strive for a consistency between thought and speech and action. The language of the Torah—or the Mayor—may sound exaggerated, but it gets the point across; when it comes to the godlike, our thoughts count. And the commandment of thought is not just a commandment to counter evil thoughts or banish them. It is an injunction to live a religious life, to create a meaningful, truthful, and just understanding of the world around us and fit our behaviors into that conceptual context. It begins inside us, with the mind and the heart. So "You can't go to jail for what you're thinking," my brother, my sister. But, as the rest of this book will try to show, the goal of life is keeping life itself from becoming like a jail, by creating a wholesome, healthy, and positive confluence of thought, speech, and action in relation to family, community, and God, by fashioning a life consistent with the universal and eternal ideals of the Ten Commandments.

Speech
What Do You Say to an Anxious Bride?

Her moment has been coming for months, his day anticipated with excitement for years. So what do you say to the nervous groom and the anxious bride? What praise might you offer if . . . well . . . uh . . . something seems amiss? What if the carefully chosen colors of the bouquet clash with the cummerbund, or if the gown is garish? What would you say if you find their perfect day to be less than absolutely perfect? The rabbis struggle with the same question, a question of thought and speech, of consistency between cogitation and communication. Our Torah demands that we

Keep far from falsehood (Exod 23:7).

What we think and what we say should be the same. Telling the groom and bride the truth seems to be important—no matter how small the matter seems to be. But to admit that the fish served for the wedding lunch was dry and cold would break their hearts. "The truth, the whole truth and nothing but the truth" *appears* to be the motto of the Ten Commandments. The Third and Ninth Commandments *seem* to demand scrupulous honesty of speech.

Let us begin our consideration of commandments of speech with Commandment Three:

27

THE TEN COMMANDMENTS

> *You shall not take the name of the Eternal, your God, in vain for the Eternal will not find guiltless the one who takes that name in vain.*

What does this mean?

Many rabbinic interpreters will tell us that this Third Commandment flatly prohibits blasphemy, the misuse of God's name. When in your hammering you strike your thumb instead of the nail, and you invoke God's name in pain, yes, it could be considered a violation of the Third Commandment. But as Abraham bar Hiyya would tell us, there is much more to the sin of speech than that.

Looking back some three thousand years, people claimed many different ways to extend human speech to a theological domain. One ancient method was divination. Long ago, people tried to "divine" God's intent through the study of natural phenomena as the toss of dice, the arrangement of a flock of birds in flight, or the pattern of liquids mixing in a divining goblet. Divination revealed whether God would make it rain or extend a drought, if people would have children, if fields would be fertile or if it was a good time to make war or declare peace. And another form of divination was in the spoken word, in incantation, in speaking magic spells, and in repeating secret chants. And this form of spoken divination is the vain use of God's name that the Ten Commandments prohibit.

In an Ancient Near East where spoken divination was a common religious practice, Israel's Ten Commandments said "Not us!" In a pagan world that sought to learn God's will secondhand by watching birds or looking into cups, Israel discerned God's intention directly from God, initially, at Sinai, and later, from reading God's books—Bible, Mishna, and Talmud. And this God who spoke to Israel condemns incantation and magic spells as sins of speech.

To the blasphemy and the divination that the Ten Commandments and subsequent traditions deride, let us add another spoken sin. In Bible times, as the Torah instructs us and the rabbis remind us, people accepted vows of asceticism. The Nazirite, for instance, "took God's name" to demonstrate a heightened level of religious intention in forsaking alcohol and sex. And the Third Commandment, scrupulously careful when it comes to God-talk, would have us be super-certain about our motives before entering a vow and the closer-to-the-Divinity status the ascetic condition carries with it. And so, a third rationale for the Third Commandment: You take God's name in vain when you make a promise to God. So, be careful when it comes to taking a spoken vow. Make promises you are sure you are going to keep.

To the rabbis, there remain four other ways to sin in speech. A person takes God's name in vain when misusing God's name to state:

1) **An obvious truth**. To swear, for instance, "By God, this table is not a horse," is to needlessly use God's name to communicate the plainly apparent.

2) **An obvious lie**. To swear, for instance, "By God, this table is a horse," is to try to lend divine credence to something that could not possibly be true. It is to apply God's name to an outlandish falsehood.

3) **The intention to commit a sin**. To swear, "By God, I am going to steal a horse," is to employ God's name in connection with the crime of theft, an action that God prohibits.

4) **The intention to do the impossible**. To swear, "By God, I am so hungry, I can eat an entire horse!" is to use God's name in a frivolous purpose, to employ divinity for something that could never happen.

So as a commandment of speech, the Third Commandment is concerned with what we say to God and how we talk about God. Whether or not we take the rabbis words literally, above all, this commandment wants us to speak with care because there is something godlike about verbal communication. More about the divinity of speech later.

Since Rabbi bar Hiyya wants us to deal with our Decalogue conceptually, we can now turn to Commandment Nine, our other commandment of speech. Where Commandment Three is concerned with speech to God, Commandment Nine considers speech in relation to people and society. It tells us

You shall not testify falsely against your neighbor.

Taken literally, it describes the importance of speaking the truth under oath, in court. Yes, our judicial testimony is so crucial that it gets its own commandment. The integrity of the community and society relies upon the soundness of the judicial system, on the impartiality of the judges, the honesty of the lawyers, and—to the Ninth Commandment—the credibility of the witnesses.

Now we might conclude that speaking to our bride and groom is just like speaking to God or speaking in court—what we say in all those cases really counts. When the Torah elsewhere commands

Keep far from falsehood (Exod 23:7),

it seems to demand we keep as far away from lying as we can. But really, what is wrong with sparing a bride's feelings with a "little white lie?" When you speak to the groom, what harm is there in "stretching the truth?" Surely, the Bible did not have these small things in mind when it commanded us to avoid lying—or did it?

I teach bio-medical ethics at the medical school in town and, like everyone in medicine, I specialize. My area is in the ethics of the "white lie." In one instance, a student described the subtlety, significance—and difficulty—in telling the whole, honest truth. A patient asked this student if the results of a medical test came back from the lab. The student happened to know that the results were in and that the report was favorable. However, hospital rules do not allow medical students to "interpret" any major test results, even good ones. Only doctors may break important news.

So what is the student to do? Let us imagine that the student decided to break the rule, give the results, and say, "You're OK." What if the patient responds with "So why does it hurt so much?" or "Do I need another test?" How should a student know how to answer those questions? Only the doctor has the training, experience, and authority to say, "You are all clear, you can go home now." The student did not want to offer the "whole" truth, that "The results are in but because I am a student, I am not allowed to share them with you. This does not indicate that the results are favorable or unfavorable." All this talk is likely to scare the patient for no good reason. And if the student responds, "I don't know," it is a lie. What is the cost of such a seemingly trivial lie? If the patient later finds out the student did know, the patient might lose respect for the student and the whole hospital. When we lie, we can get caught, even in a little one.

The class was stymied. It is wrong to lie, and the student can neither answer the question nor explain why no answer can be given. One student suggested the following response: "Let me get someone to interpret the results for you. I will be right back." And the group determined that this response made the best of an awkward situation. The white lie was avoided, and the patient would get the necessary information quickly with the integrity of the student and the institution affirmed and protected. But when we get to the wedding reception, should we hold our speech to the same standard of truth?

After all, the white lie is ingrained in our culture. What is exactly wrong with telling a cop, "I was speeding because I have a stomach cramp and I have to get home fast." What harm is there in the note signed "with fondness" that is sent to someone you hope you never see again? Is it a sin when a world political leader puts a little "spin" on the news to protect the national interest? Shading the truth has become so common that the white lie is almost a national institution.

The rabbis debate the nature of the little lie in the Talmud (*Ketubot*, 16b-17a). Going back to our bride and groom, the Rabbi, Shammai, tells us that one is obligated to, "Tell them exactly what you see," no matter how disappointing or upsetting, trivial or substantial." On the other hand, Rabbi Hillel, the more lenient of the two rabbis, wants us to tell the truth—but not necessarily all of it. Later sages come to the conclusion that Shammai is wrong, Hillel is right, and we are to conduct ourselves "in a pleasant manner." So if the dress or tux is aesthetically lacking, then find something nice to say about the flowers or the table setting. Taken together, the thoughts of my students and the rabbis lead me to conclude that we are not to lie to the bride and we are not to express the brutal truth either. Instead, we are to find something truthful to say.

With the few words, "Let there be light," according to the Torah, God created the universe. Speech has that much creative power. And in our wedding halls, in our houses of worship, and in our courts, our speech becomes as creative and as important as God's, every word of it. With words we, too, fashion a universe. Look what happens to the relationships and the society filled with white lies—distrust and cynicism overwhelm them. When we regularly distort reality to spare people's feelings, we will never know whether or not to believe one another. Such is the power of our truthful—or untruthful—speech. Yes, there is something godlike in our words, when we create a harmony of thinking, speaking, and doing. All this as our next chapter turns to action, mother and father, husband and wife.

Family, Parents, and Spouse
The Human Stepstool

The poor college student was in emotional torment. His heart told him to declare himself an art major. His parents demanded he enter a course of study leading to a more conventional way to earn a living. With vacation and intersession looming—a month at home with the family after a week of angry phone calls—he feared the upcoming school break would become one, long painful argument.

I was assigned to be his counselor, myself only several years after the completion of rabbinic studies, myself a student in a graduate school of social work. This young man in conflict was my "client" and he summed up his dilemma in these words, "Should I listen to my parents and do what *they* think is right? Or should I listen to myself and do what *I* think is right?"

The budding social worker in *me* told me to listen to my supervisor and help the student "individuate," to assist him in setting his own life course. "Lead him to see and describe his situation," she said. "Help him talk about his own wishes for himself. Guide him to react to the demands his parents are making of him. Don't give him any answers. Give him time to express himself."

But after reading our Fifth Commandment of family, the rabbi in me might well regard my supervisor's advice as a violation of

> *Honor your father and your mother that you live many days on the land God gives you.*

If my "client" does what his parents want him to do, if he declares an engineering major, then, according to the Torah, he should be set for life. If "Do your own thing" is what he decides, if he goes into art, he will pay a price. Simply stated, the loyalty we owe the God who freed us from slavery in Egypt is the loyalty we owe the parents who brought us into adulthood. But do the Ten Commandments *really* want us to follow our parents automatically, without question?

The rabbis interpret the Fifth Commandment to demand two things of adult children. First of all, to the rabbis, the Fifth Commandment expects a grown child to provide for a parent's material needs—food, shelter, and clothing—and physical safety as well. A child is to ensure that a parent suffers no material want. Second, the rabbis tell us, an adult child must respect a parent in public. For instance, one should not embarrass or contradict a parent in front of others. "Food, shelter, and clothing," and "Praise in public and criticize in private," appear to be the first and second legs of the rabbinic sense of this Fifth Commandment. But is that all there is? Does not "honor" mean "obey"?

> When Rabbi Tarfon's mother wished to climb into bed, the Rabbi would bend down and let his mother use him as a step. When she climbed out of bed, she again used him as a step. When Rabbi Tarfon boasted of this in the Rabbinic Academy, his colleagues replied, "You have not yet reached half the honor due her . . ." (*Talmud Kiddushin*, 31b)

Yes, the Talmud wants us to bend to suit the wishes of our parents, but do we owe them our unquestioning obedience under all circumstances? Do we honor Mom and Dad by literally, like Tarfon, becoming the human

FAMILY, PARENTS, AND SPOUSE

stepstool and letting them walk all over us? And even then, is that only half the honor due them?

Sometimes the rabbis speak with a sense of humor—a little pulling of the leg. Sometimes the rabbis exaggerate their arguments, and sometimes they pepper their lessons with a couple of chuckles and I think this is one of those times. By relating this story, Rabbi Tarfon shows he takes the Torah's word to the extreme. And his rabbinic colleagues teased him with their response, "You have not yet reached . . ."

So I could turn to my student, as a social worker, even as a rabbi, and say the same thing. "Honor your mother and father" means "respect" and it means "listen carefully and consider." It does not mean reacting in a knee-jerk, automatic, mindless fashion. "Honoring" means communicating with decency and love. After studying my student's situation and the Jewish tradition, I recognized that my supervisor advised me well.

When we come to commandments of family, sometimes the rabbis add a shade of meaning to the Torah's text. "Honor" does not mean unquestioning obedience. It means caring and respecting. But before we further consider the possibility of what may seem like "stretching" the intent of the Decalogue, we turn from the Fifth Commandment to the Seventh Commandment, the other "family value."

We read:

You shall not commit adultery.

Shortly after I earned my social work degree, I began to read books about the "how-to" of psycho-therapy. I found a book that describes a counselor's efforts to aid a couple on the edge of divorce. It seems that the husband had been carrying on a secret affair—until the wife found out and became furious. He told his wife that the other woman meant nothing to him, that she, his wife, was first and foremost, forever. His wife, in response, accused him of poor morals and said she wanted out of the marriage. At an impasse, they both came to the therapist, who made the following suggestion to the wife:

"Why don't you have an affair, too, in order to even things out? Then, when the score is even, we can begin to have a meaningful talk."

The therapist's stated goals? Restore the balance, regain a marital parity. If both perform adultery, if both become faithless, there will be common ground, and the two wrongs will make it right.

First, I went to seminary to become a rabbi. Then I went to a school of social work, knowing that at some point, what they told me in seminary would not necessarily agree with what they would tell me in social work school. Here we have a clear case of it. The Ten Commandments *command* us:

> *You shall not commit adultery.*

and would never approve of adultery, even if one's spouse already did it, even if it did save a marriage. As we saw in the earlier chapters, the Ten Commandments set out a categorical imperative to apply to all people, in all places, and at all times. You can *think* about adultery because "Brother, you can't go to jail for what you're thinking." But doing it is a different matter altogether. And I know many psychotherapists, let alone rabbis, who would make my case with me.

Sometimes it is acceptable, even good, believe it or not, to desecrate a commandment, even one of the Ten. By unanimous vote of the rabbis, the need to attend to a person in a life-threatening situation—drowning, fire, heart attack—supersedes any of the Sabbath's prohibitions. "Break the law to save a life" is a religious obligation any day of the week.

FAMILY, PARENTS, AND SPOUSE

Now let us pursue how the rabbis approach the statement that "two wrongs make a right." The rabbis invent an interesting situation. Suppose a parent asks a child to desecrate the Sabbath in non-life-threatening circumstances. Let's say it is a Saturday and parents tell a child to run down to the supermarket for a quart of milk. Here the child is in a bind. If the child says, "Yes, Mom and Dad, whatever you say, I'll do," the child desecrates the Sabbath—violates the Fourth Commandment—but keeps the Fifth Commandment to honor parents. If the child says, "No!" to Mom and Dad, the child keeps the Sabbath, but defies his or her parents and violates the Fifth Commandment. Either way the child loses. The rabbis respond to the problem with the following advice: keep the Sabbath and honor God, the higher authority.

So sometimes it is proper to desecrate the Sabbath, for instance, if a life is at stake. And sometimes it is proper to disobey parents, for instance, if parents ask us to violate a higher law. But, "What about the prohibition of adultery? Is adultery ever allowed?" What if a therapist thinks adultery is a good way to restore balance to an already damaged marital relationship? Isn't saving a marriage more important than some archaic list of obsolete commandments? Isn't marital fidelity an ethical dinosaur? I heard just this argument when I was teaching a local Elderhostel.

"Rabbi, adultery is everywhere. In politics, on TV, it seems every one is doing it. Look Rabbi, if the man and the woman both agree, then where is the crime? And what about the husband of a woman who has advanced Alzheimer's? He visits her daily in the nursing home. Are you telling us he ought to divorce his wife in order to be with someone else and live a little bit? Rabbi, be reasonable. This is the modern era. If the adults are freely consenting, then there is no victim."

These people were, thirty, forty years my senior. And they made me look like the anachronism, like the prude. But look at our Torah and how the rabbis reiterate the prohibition of adultery, equating it with idolatry and murder:

> Raba said in Rabbi Yohanan's name: We may save ourselves with all forbidden things except idolatry, sexual misconduct and murder . . . One came before Raba and said: The Governor of my town has ordered me, "Go kill so-and-so. If not I will kill you." He answered: "He should kill you rather than you should commit murder. What reason do you see for thinking that your blood is redder? Perhaps his blood is redder?" (*Talmud Pesahim* 25a, also see *Sanhedrin* 74a).

Of all the Torah's 613 commandments, the precepts concerning idolatry, sexual misconduct, and murder are the most difficult to find an excuse to break. Yes, if the husband's adultery is wrong, then more adultery, even by a jilted wife at the recommendation of a psychotherapist, is also wrong.

Now perhaps the therapist did not really mean it, perhaps it was the therapist's goal to "stoke the coals," open a new level of communication between the man and the woman by suggesting a powerful, provocative, worst case, "What if?" Perhaps he did not really expect her to have an affair; perhaps he only wanted them to imagine something outlandish. Maybe the therapist wanted to pull their leg like the rabbis pulled ours when they answered that braggart Tarfon.

I would answer the therapist as a therapist. A relationship must be built on mutual, unshakable trust, not mutual infidelity. Trying to build a positive relationship on a negative behavior will probably and eventually pull the people apart.

FAMILY, PARENTS, AND SPOUSE

To the Torah, fidelity between husband and wife strengthens the family and thus strengthens society. Marital trust builds a stable environment for the children and sets the scene for a sound economic, cultural and social underpinning for the home. When we considered commandments of thought and speech, we stressed the consistency of thinking and speaking. And with commandments of family and action, we bring our deeds into that crucial consistency and move to a broader picture still.

"The Torah's always telling us to do this or do that for this one or for that one. You know, Rabbi, look at the Ten Commandments. They want us to honor parents, keep the Sabbath—for God—and do all these things for other people. Where does the Torah tell you to take time for yourself?"

The question came from a hard-driving and successful executive in the Torah study class at the suburban New York, Westchester County congregation, where I served as a freshly minted rabbi. And that week, he confronted me, or should I say, I confronted myself with his pivotal question.

This executive and most of the others in the group had probably attended more Torah study sessions as students than I had the experience handling as a teacher. I turned to the rest of the group, and asked, "What do you think?" hoping someone would venture an answer to his question and bail me out. Instead, we all listened to a silence that I knew I had to fill.

"The Jewish tradition wants us to pay more attention to others than we do to ourselves," I finally heard myself say. "Oh, there are a few exceptions. For instance, Rabbi Hillel told us, 'If I am not for myself, who will be for me?' Which seems to tell us that we come first. But he also said, 'If I am for myself alone, what am I?' which means that even if I put myself first, I still have an obligation to you."

"And look at the Sabbath commandment. On the surface, it looks as if we keep it in order to get a day of rest. But really, it is a commandment to imitate God, to stop work after six days, just the way God stopped work after six days of creation. It is not commanding us to relax or to feel good. Maybe you can find a commandment or two that tell us to take care of ourselves, for ourselves alone. But I guarantee, they are in the minority."

From the look on his face, I knew I did not convince him. But by now, I had convinced myself. As Jews, our Covenant demands we reach out to others, not in to ourselves. We do not always come first. We meet our needs as a by-product, as a side effect of meeting the needs of family, community, and God.

Back in the 1970s, posters bearing "The Gestalt Prayer" appeared on college dormitory walls as plentifully as blue denim across a campus green. The "Gestalt Prayer," written by the late Fritz Perls, pillar of Gestalt psychotherapy, reads

> I do my thing and you do your thing. I am not in this world to live up to your expectation and you are not in this world to live up to mine. You are you and I am I. And if by chance we find each other, it's beautiful. If not, it can't be helped.

The Gestalt prayer declared, "Live and let live. You do your thing and let me do mine. We owe nothing to one another." Compare the Gestalt prayer, "Myself alone and forever," to the words of the Ten Commandments and their call for loyalty to family, community, and God. Others—spouse, family and as we will see in the next chapter, community, just in the order Abraham bar Hiyya set for us—are our highest priority.

Community
A History of Strangers and the Responsibility of Redeemers

At first, I thought the old adage "Right pew, wrong church," described me, a rabbi teaching a course on Judaism in the classroom of a Catholic college. But it took me half a semester to realize that the Catholic college was the "right church" as well. After covering the Jewish basics—holidays, customs, history, philosophy, and the like—I asked my students to complete a take-home examination whose last test question called for a description of the origins of Jewish ethics. I expected the typical student's response to look like this:

> What we call Jewish ethics has its origins in Exodus and later books of the Torah where, for a total of forty-four times, Scripture demands that Jews protect the stranger because the Jewish people were themselves strangers and slaves in Egypt. The Bible mentions no other commandment as frequently as the commandment about the stranger, no other commandments about holidays, the Sabbath, faith in God, marriage, circumcision, or anything else.
>
> Jews must remember and ponder their slavery; each Jew is to think of himself or herself as having been enslaved and redeemed. And the Bible insists that Jews are not to make slaves of their strangers the way the

45

> Egyptians enslaved them. Furthermore, the Bible demands that they safeguard and love the stranger the way their God who loved them displayed that love by freeing the Jews from Egypt.
>
> The Torah, and later the rabbis, broaden the category of "stranger," establishing a protected social class of human beings, including the widow and the orphan. Though powerless, they all are nevertheless fashioned in God's image, and the Jew is obligated to protect them. Jewish philosopher Martin Buber said that we judge the goodness of a society by examining the way it treats its powerless. And only a society that looks out for the well being of its powerless can be called good. And this is the basis of Jewish ethics.

I took the pile of exams and sat in a cozy family-room chair, excited to read my first written papers for my first college course. I expected to savor the sweet first fruits of the budding intellect, nothing less than some divine revelation. But after an hour, I found myself boring through a pile of unimaginative retreads of my own words and I quickly came to recognize the reality of academic life. A lecture hall of stuffy air and dozing students adds up to twenty nearly identical papers. I read my way to the bottom of the pile, until one student's words jarred me:

> You would think the Jewish people would be embarrassed about having been slaves, that they would want to blot it out like a prison record and never talk about it again. Instead, they are proud of their enslavement. Slavery is not a source of embarrassment but the source of Jewish ethics.

That student was absolutely right and I had never looked at it that way before! All those Passover Seders where I read, that, "Each one of us is to feel as if he, as if she was a slave in the land of Egypt, every one of us freed from imprisonment in the house of bondage." I had to make myself into a stranger, a Jew in Christian surroundings and I had to have someone outside my faith show me how proud I am of my painful beginning!

We were strangers in Egypt, strangers even before that in Canaan. We began with one couple, Abraham and Sarah, who left their home and homeland on the promise of an invisible God. They journeyed across the Near East desert, nomads in search of Canaan. There they grew from a small family into a small community.

As desert wanderers, we were strangers to everyone we met. Our name, *ivri*, meaning "Hebrew," literally means "from the other side." That was our beginning—as a people from someplace else.

Years later, Joseph, the great-grandson of Sarah and Abraham, himself originally a stranger in Egypt, was jailed for a crime he did not commit. Joseph quickly rose from prison to become King Pharaoh's second in command in the land. During a time of famine Joseph literally fed the nation of Egypt, managing the nation's foodstocks and sparing the population from starvation. And the rest of Joseph's family joined him in Egypt.

As a small Hebrew community within a larger Egyptian community, we quickly grew in number, but the Egyptians always saw us as strangers. Then a new king came to power in Egypt. This new Egyptian monarch feared we would organize a grassroots rebellion, "rise from the land," to ally ourselves with a foreign enemy, challenge Pharaoh and make the Egyptians into strangers in their own homeland. The Egyptians impressed us into national service, conscripting us as state slaves for national public works projects. Then our God redeemed us, as we read in the opening of the Ten Commandments. And instead of being a source of embarrassment, our slavery has become the source of our communal ethics.

THE TEN COMMANDMENTS

See how we constantly remind ourselves and the world that we were slaves. We speak of our servitude in our daily prayers, weekly Sabbath worship, festival celebration, and in the Ten Commandments. And we teach our children of our enslavement and our redemption, just as our Torah commands us to do. The bondage to freedom story is a crucial component of Jewish faith.

The very first commandment of our Decalogue tells us that

> *I am the Eternal, your God, who brought you out of the land of Egypt, from a house of bondage.*

And if this prominence in the Bible's Exodus version of the Ten Commandments is not enough, we recall our tour in chains later on in the Bible's Deuteronomy, in the fourth commandment, as the reason for the Sabbath:

> *Remember that you were a slave in the land of Egypt*
> (Deut 5:15)

And some forty-two more times the Bible reiterates our slave experience to conclude:

> *You shall not oppress the stranger, you know the spirit of the stranger, because you were strangers in the land of Egypt.*
> (Exod 23:9)

Our ordeal as strangers and the stunning tale of the redemption are the keynote of Jewish community, history, theology, society, and celebration.

As much as our history as strangers is the centerpiece of Judaism, the world is getting tired of hearing us talk about our hard times—the years in Egypt, the destruction of two Temples in Israel, pogroms and above all, the Holocaust. For three millennia, we were driven from our homes and our homelands, oppressed as strangers on and off, and it seems Jew and non-Jew have had enough of that story. "We suffered as much, if not more than you did," some non-Jews respond to us as if we vie with them in a shouting match for bragging rights for the medal that honors "The World's Greatest Victim." And if your patience too is thinning, may I beg your indulgence once more because we have yet to adequately communicate the real lesson of our experience.

Not long ago I saw a movie about the cliche of the young, savvy professional who left the pressures of New York urban existence for what she expected would be a new and easier life in a small town in rural New England. A sophisticated big city corporate lawyer who never lost a dime on a client's deal, as soon as she moved into her new home in the woods, she was the quick and easy prey of local business operators—the real estate agent, the lawyer, the heating oil dealer, the home improvement contractor who colluded to betray her trust and take her money. In New York, on her own turf, she was in total control. But in New England, unfamiliar with the ways of country life, she was easy prey with no one to stand up for her. An onlooker might conclude the local version of this small town Bible reads, "You once were strangers. Now that you are the small town local, the next stranger to walk into your homeland shall be your prey."

Actually, there were two kinds of non-citizens, or strangers, in Bible times. The first is the "foreigner," *nochri* or *zar*, in Hebrew, who traveled abroad with a foreign national allegiance and carried around the invisible protection of the folks back home. To speak in more contemporary terms, when I have traveled abroad, when I strolled past an American embassy, among my feelings of homesickness and pride I also felt a measure of safety. If I fell ill or ran out of money, I could turn to the American embassy for help. And the *zar*, the foreigner back in Bible times, felt like I did. When the *zar* ran into trouble, the *zar* had a place to turn to.

The second non-citizen was the *ger*, the "stranger." When abroad, the "stranger" did not have the security I enjoyed. The *ger* had no national allegiance to a homeland. Without state ties, the stranger lacked a safe haven in a distant land. Where the foreigner, like me, had someplace to turn for help, the defenseless stranger, on the other hand, had none. The New York lawyer in my example from the movie, the *ger*, without a passport or embassy to turn to, with no one to stand behind her, became the exploited stranger.

The Bible looks back on our history as strangers in Egypt and expands the category "stranger" to include all those of our community without the protection of parent, guardian or spouse. The stranger becomes more than a wayfarer "without a country." The stranger becomes the widow and the orphan, and the hungry, as we were, alone in an uncaring and cold, hard world. The homeless without a landholding, the unemployed without means of earning a livelihood, the Torah considers them strangers, too. The Torah's stranger is anyone caught in the cogs of society for reasons beyond their control. We know what it is like to be the working single parent trying to finish school, the father holding down two shifts to make ends meet, the mother who earns little more than the cost of child care. So the Bible concludes:

> *You shall not oppress the stranger. You know the spirit of the stranger because you were strangers in the land of Egypt* (Exod 23:9).

Not just us, not just then, but all powerless people for all time. Protecting the stranger is our first responsibility.

I imagine myself living long ago as an Egyptian, seeing myself reading the last few paragraphs. I would be tempted to cry out, "Hey, we Egyptians are not a bunch of vultures flying circles and drooling over some dying animal. In this cruel world where only a few make it, we are just trying to survive. We are victims, too, you know. Where is a little sympathy for us?"

Truth is, many essentially good-hearted and decent people are responsible for much evil, all in the name of making it to the end of the day in an environment they see as vicious and hostile. "We really don't want to make you into slaves," they eventually might have said to us. "We were just trying to protect ourselves and insure our fair share and survival," shout the New England townspeople and the leaders of Egypt. "Let these weaklings learn how to protect themselves. And if they don't know how to protect themselves, let them learn the hard way just like we learned—if they ever learn at all."

It is a great distance from ancient Egypt to the contemporary social and political scene but, three thousand years later, we hear again and again, "We are on a lifeboat tossing in a fierce storm, with too many would-be survivors scrambling to climb aboard for the too few seats to safety. If we let everyone on, if we try to carry all the social stragglers and every economic misfit, if we are joined by all those who would harm us intentionally or unintentionally, then all of us will drown. We mighty will become feeble if we try to save the very weak. Instead of offering compassion for the less fortunate who will eventually falter anyway, we would best perform a triage, pick out the most likely survivors, cut loose the weaker and let them drown now. Why waste our limited and precious resources? So let us push aside the feeble and look out for ourselves."

In a world of corporate downsizing and cost cutting, the prudent management slogans like "It's dog eat dog," abound. We hear how "The big fish swallows the smaller" and "It's the law of the jungle." And even in this cruel atmosphere, the Torah demands that we distinguish between zoology and spirituality, between the litany of "survival of the fittest . . . get them before they get you," and the imperative of God's covenanted community.

I was eighteen years old, a high school senior, when I read *The Stranger* by Albert Camus. The last question of our final English exam asked, "Why was the book called *The Stranger?*" I thought of the main character, and without really understanding what I was saying I wrote, "Because Meursault was a stranger to himself." You could imagine my surprise when I received the full ten points for the question and a "Good Answer!" as well. But it took the next eighteen years of my life to really understand. It is many hundreds of miles from Egypt to Algiers and millennia from Meursault, a stranger in Algiers, to Moses, a stranger in Egypt, and myself in a Brooklyn high school or a Western Massachusetts synagogue. But in any of these places, the answer is the same.

We still personalize the story of the exodus, not as some long ago history textbook experience, but as immediate and right now. Each one of us, you and I, were there in Egypt, together shackled and redeemed. The last player picked for the touch football team, the only one in the senior class facing graduation without a job—each time we experience an estrangement, no matter how small or large, it takes us back to the time we were slaves. And when we protect and help the stranger we reenact our own redemption from Egypt.

Today's stranger tosses sleepless in bed while the rest of the house—and it seems the world—sleeps at peace. The stranger is alone on Yom Kippur, the Jewish Day of Atonement, although standing in a crowd, is alone before God in judgment, bereft of excuses or defenders, facing misdeeds and the Maker, alone before history and the future. The stranger is the young soldier on the battlefront hearing echoes of explosions in the distance and the stranger is the child worried that nuclear war will annihilate all humanity. And the stranger is the victim of the drip-drip of day-in, day-out pollution that wears away the topsoil and depletes the atmosphere of life sustaining air in the slow withering of our home planet.

Yes, the Bible is right when it reminds us:

You know the spirit of the stranger.

We know about slavery. We know all about working day and night without an end to the work, without a goal or feelings of accomplishment, where the morning light dawns on another day in the endless chain of labor. In Egypt, the human became the beast of burden, whose back bore the taskmasters whip and the blazing sun. During what the rabbis say were our four hundred years of bondage, the soul was beaten out of us, our bodies bruised and our spirit broken. Yes, we know the heart of the stranger, but we focus not on enslavement but redemption, not on pain but on freedom, not on what the Egyptians did *to* us but what God did *for* us and what we are to do today. Looking beyond the Bible, our sages offer a full array of responses from economic, to legal, to psychological, to show the importance of caring for the stranger.

From an economic standpoint, one of our earliest rabbinic sources, the *Mechilta of Rabbi Ishmael, looks at the Bible's verse:*

You shall not oppress the stranger (Exod 22:20)

and applies it "to money matters." The economic ethic of caring for the stranger prohibits taking unfair financial advantage of the defenseless worker who does not enjoy the power and protection that comes from owning wealth. For instance, as might a union rule book, the Torah demands that the employer pay the laborer at the end of the work day and not hold an employee's money beyond when the salary is due. The Torah demands that we not take the neighbor's last garment as pledge. The Torah is not a radical socialist manifesto; Scripture holds no grudge against people who have money. Rather, the ethic of the Jewish tradition concerns itself with the way we use any power that our possessions offer us, that we do not exploit those who have less.

Our history saw us live under laws that excluded us, prevented us from getting an education, from owning and working the land, denied us the practice of our professions and closed our businesses, all because we were Jews. But our Torah guarantees the stranger equal protection under Jewish civil law. Our biblical government is established on the principle:

You shall have one law for stranger and citizen alike (Lev 24:22).

Under the rules of our land, the Ten Commandments and the Bible extend the protection of the civil law to stranger and citizen. While there are some exceptions for religious practice, the homeborn and the stranger enjoy equivalent legal protection and benefit.

Just as we had one law for all in our lawbooks across the land, our judges enforced one law for all in the courts. The commentator Bechor Shor applied

And you shall not oppress a stranger (Exod 23:9)

to the workings of the court system, calling upon us not "to deal unfairly with the stranger's case." Leviticus later enjoins, "You shall not render an unfair decision, do not favor the poor or show deference to the rich." In matters of money, property, public behavior, labor, or the protection of life and limb, the Bible demanded that our community of former slaves use its power and authority to treat stranger and homeborn in the same way.

COMMUNITY

On a psychological level, we offer emotional comfort. "You shall not vex the stranger," means you shall not taunt "with words," the *Mechilta* explains. We are not to use the ability of speech to harm feelings. Instead of teasing the stranger, we speak words of consolation. Yes, we pledge not to make sport or a dollar off the newcomer—and we are to go even further.

The Covenant of the Ten Commandments envisions for itself a community whose thoughts, speech, and deeds are directed toward protecting the powerless. Yet, often I will hear people say, "My own religion—the rules I live my life by—is not an organized religion. It is a religion of myself. My personal creed tells me not to hurt anyone, to mind my own business but be honest and fair and never cheat, lie or steal. And if I manage to take care of myself and not hurt anyone, then I am doing fine." But to the Covenant of the Ten Commandments, this is not enough.

To the Torah, to leave the stranger alone to starve or freeze to death is inadequate. We are above all commanded to treat the stranger the way God treated us and not treat others the way we were mistreated. "With an outstretched arm and a mighty hand" God redeemed us and we have to follow God's example and tell our children and grandchildren about our experience, demanding that they do the same. It's not enough not to harm—we have to help, individually and collectively, as private citizens and as a society as a whole. We are commanded to remember that we were mistreated and victimized and we channel that frustration into a pledge—when we come into our own power, we exercise that power with compassion for the widow, the stranger and the orphan, all those whom life dealt a bad hand. "I will not let anyone else go through what I had to suffer." We are to follow God's example and stand up for all of society's disempowered.

We could look back on those four hundred years under Pharaoh and tell ourselves we were badly wounded and scarred by our bondage. We could have spent the subsequent forty years of wandering through Sinai spewing anger at those who enslaved us, venting regret for all the time we wasted piling bricks. But our Ten Commandments open with:

> *I am the Eternal, your God, who brought you out of the land of Egypt, from a house of bondage,*

telling us to think of God and the redemption when we recall our times as strangers. We do not waste our freedom plotting a counter attack against Egypt, getting even for the years we spent in suffering. Instead we move our emotions ahead to a land flowing with milk and honey, our attitude shaped by the promise of new life in a rich land.

What we tell ourselves about the things that go on around us, how we react to our suffering and how we interpret our joy, all these are evidence the attitude we take toward the conditions of life. We respond positively and we affirm, through thought, speech and action, the potential for goodness in the world despite hardship.

The Torah calls upon us not to stand by idly while a human being suffers, to rise to the aid of the elderly, the lost, the ill, all in need, to build a redeeming, godlike society under the rules of ethical monotheism. In Bible times, we fed the hungry by guaranteeing them access to the fields after the harvest. We let them glean the fields clean of the produce we left behind. We fight ignorance, political oppression, and homelessness. We are not obligated to spend society's last dollars in this effort; we are to undertake a good faith try to help. Such is our covenanted responsibility in contemporary terms. As a covenanted community, each one of us bears a responsibility to imitate the God who helped us when we were in need. We take on God's role and redeem others the way God redeemed us.

So now, let us ask a fundamental question, lurking in the background of these five chapters. Just who is this God who spoke to Moses out of the burning bush, who struck Pharaoh's land with ten plagues and split the sea so we could safely flee across dry land and escape our pursuers? Just what do we mean when we speak the word, "God?"

6

God
The Cosmic 800 Number and Divine Next Day Mail

"Sometimes God's . . . not nice," observed Kristi Pflanz, a West Des Moines, Iowa second grader. "[Once God disappointed us with] this machine where you try . . . [to use a mechanical arm] to grab a stuffed animal. God didn't give us luck on that . . . Four dollars in quarters . . . and we didn't get any stuffed animals."

The writer of a *Life* magazine cover story called, "God," spoke to a cross section of people on just that topic. And many of those interviewed offered the same anger, frustration, and disappointment—and more—as Kristi. Why pray to a God who does not answer prayer, a Deity who seems to ignore us and our heartfelt concerns? When we implore God for an end to an illness and a return to good health, and those prayers get no answer or get "No" for an answer, we may, like Kristi, also conclude, "Sometimes God's not nice."

When Pharaoh enslaved us, we cried out to our God who heard us and rescued us. When we were in need back then, God came to our aid with a mighty hand and an outstretched arm. Today, our pleas for peace or healing seem to get God's cold shoulder. Where did all the miracles go? Is the saving God of the

Bible angry with us? Is God bored with us? Or are these old Bible stories nothing more than glorified fables? Was there any God to begin with . . .?

Many of the faithful trust in God's omniscience, omnipotence, omnipresence, and benevolence. An omniscient God who knows all is aware of our deepest thoughts, our hidden emotions, hopes, plans, and worries. An omnipotent God is capable of doing all, from halting the sun in its path, to splitting the seas, to changing the direction of a mighty river's flow. An omnipresent God is everywhere, an influence in every corner of the universe. And a benevolent God cares for us like the compassionate, caring God whose miracles redeemed us from slavery. So, to many believers, when we face illness or difficulty in our business or family, God knows about our plight, wants to offer aid and has the resources to help us out of our modern-day predicament. And sometimes it seems God does give us what we pray for. But so often, we come away from prayer empty-handed, lamenting as Kristi did, "God's not nice."

Now we enter into our discussion the Second Commandment and its consideration of the sin of idolatry:

> *I Adonai, your God, am a jealous God, holding children accountable for the sins of parents to three, to four generations of those who spurn me.*

Believe it or not Kristi, according to the Second of the Ten Commandments, your sorry lot could well be a punishment for the sins of your ancestors! God is punishing them by punishing you!

Sounds absurd, doesn't it? A God so jealous and vengeful, a God who inflicted punishment down through the generations. And the Torah uses the specific example of the sin of idolatry! Just what's so bad with saying a few prayers to a rock?

GOD

"It bothers me too," if I might paraphrase Nahmanides and ibn Ezra, for example, two of our classical rabbinic commentators. (*Ramban* to Exod 20:5). "But that's just what happened. When the sinner is a parent, God leaves the parent alone and punishes the child. And, if after punishing the child there remains punishment still to be had, then God works down to the third, even forth generation." To Nahmanides

> *Holding children accountable for the sins of parents means just what it says.*

Nahmanides was satisfied with the cold explanations of inherited guilt and inherited punishment. But other rabbis were not and did their best to try to "explain away" the deep discomfort they felt about the injustice of the Second Commandment. Some rabbis recast the harsh Second Commandment as a form of disguised compassion. They point to the Talmud, which tells us that children suffer for their parents only when the offspring followed in their parents' misguided footsteps. (*Talmud Sanhedrin*, 27b) When children behave righteously, they break the chain of intergenerational sin, God forgives and the young are spared. Who said, "God's not nice?" To the Talmud, God's very nice—once people stop misbehaving. When there is repentance, a whole-hearted turning away from sin, our very forgiving God forgoes the need to punish.

Medieval commentator Rabbi Abraham ibn Ezra agrees (Exod 20:5). Our patient and compassionate God does not punish the idolater directly or immediately, but graciously waits in hope that the sinner will mend those evil ways and repent—and no punishment will have to be meted out. And if a wicked parent somehow raises a righteous child, the memory of the misdeed can be erased and the whole sinful business forgotten. "God's not nice?" God is doing the sinner a favor by offering a second chance. Not *nice enough* for you? Then also consider this from ibn Ezra. To paraphrase him, "God may punish the third generation and the fourth generation—but not the fifth. Even God is not *that* vengeful." Eventually the inherited guilt goes away. Five generations and the slate is cleansed. What at first blush seems unforgiving and bad is, in reality, quite compassionate and good—according to ibn Ezra.

To ibn Ezra, to Rashi and to many people today, there are two sides to God and life, *reward* and *punishment*. To look at our pain without considering all of our blessings leads us to take God's stricter side out of context. "Consider the whole picture, Kristi," these thinkers would say. "Look at what you have, what God has given you. God blessed you with four dollars in quarters to begin with. You see the half-full cup as half empty." And so, Rashi, (Exod 20:6) who claims that, yes, when it comes to sin, God punishes down to

> *three, to four generations*

but he sees the half-full cup when it comes to righteousness, God is

> *kind to the thousandth generation of those who love Me and keep My commandments.*

See Kristi—God harbors many more generations of love than vengeance! And look at the sin of the Second Commandment!

Idolatry may not sound like much of a sin by today's standards, but to the Bible and our rabbis, idol worship is far from what we might today consider "a victimless crime." Idolatry meant more than offering a burnt offering to a hunk of carved wood. Idolatry frequently included sexual practices as part of its worship, possibly temple prostitution, even child sacrifice, heinous acts to a Bible that abhorred adultery and sexual misconduct and protected its young.

Perhaps the Torah was justified in coming down so strongly on the issue of idolatry. But the Second Commandment still leaves me with two challenging theological questions:

1) Does God "visit the sins of the parent on the child?"
2) Does God "visit guilt" at all?

How on earth can a just and compassionate God punish children for the sins of parents? Even the Bible itself sees a need to revise its own theology. In Exodus, the child suffers for the wrongdoing of the adult. But when we move ahead to later books of the Bible, to the Bible's Deuteronomy (24:16) we see that

> *parents shall not be put to death for the sins of their children nor shall the child die for the sins of their parents. One shall die for one's own sin.*

and the prophet Ezekiel (18:20) claims that only

> *The one who sins will die. The child shall not bear the consequences of the parent's sin nor the parent bear the consequences of the child's sin. The righteous shall bear their own righteousness and the evil their own wickedness.*

The Bible itself eventually recognizes the blatant injustice of penalizing a person for the misdeed of someone else, even if that someone else is a blood relative. So what did the commandment have in mind when it warned us of God's

> *holding children accountable for the sins of parents to three, to four generations of those who spurn me.*

What did it mean then and what does it teach us today?

First, let us note an important difference between the way we live now and the way people lived back then. In Bible times, it was not unusual for three or four generations of family to live together under one roof, or in the case of our Bible ancestors, under one tent. It was not unusual in Bible times to find a two-year-old child, with sixteen-year-old parents, thirty-year-old grandparents and forty-two-year-old great-grandparents all in one household. The family lived together as one.

In a society where one did not make a go of life alone, when one person sinned, the entire household paid the price. When the whole family is so tightly connected, when someone gets sick or hurt or does something wrong, each individual family member carries the burden, firsthand and to the person. Why does punishment end with the fourth generation? Where was the fifth generation?—People did not live long enough for the generations to stretch out so far. That would explain why the Bible stops at four generations of punishment; the fifth is not born yet.

Second, we have to distinguish between a *consequence* and a *punishment*. Throw a rock at a window and the glass breaks—shattered glass is a consequence of the flying rock that someone chose to hurl. The rock did not come from God—it came from someone who chose to throw it. The shattered pane is a consequence, a result of a human being making a toss. In the same way, what happens in life—good or bad—does not come from God. Illness, success, health, economic hardship, rain in its season, tornadoes, sunny days and earthquakes, life's good fortunes and misfortunes, good and bad, are all consequences of human choices or the normal workings of nature. And is collective responsibility any different for us today? The social crimes, adultery, murder, theft, perjury, even graffiti, drug abuse, and the like, all have a collective consequence. When one member of a group dies, all the members are affected. A mugging, marital infidelity, false testimony in court, all drag society down, compromising the communal good. When one person sins, the entire community suffers. And that's how all pay—on some level—for the sin of one.

This lesson on family consequences came to me not long ago when three generations of an extended family of recent Jewish emigrants from the former Soviet Union joined us for dinner in our home—children the age of ours, parents a little younger than we and grandparents a little younger than our parents. As we ate, they described the consequences of moving across the world. The family spoke of professional compromises. Well trained by Soviet standards, their skills were not up to par in America. And with additional issues of language and culture, they were forced to accept employment at the lower end of the earnings spectrum, far lower than they knew in the former Soviet Union. They described themselves and other émigrés, former teachers now working as day care providers and nursery school aides, former building construction engineers now changing oil at a car repair shop or working as custodians, former doctors returning to school to become recertified and former dentists supporting themselves as hygienists. There was family back in Russia, relatives they knew they would never see again. No, they are not sorry they came. They knew all this came with life in America.

After dinner, once our guests left, as my wife, Debbie, and I talked about the evening, we came to recognize the significant inter-generational consequences of family decisions. Had their family chosen to come to America some hundred years ago instead of ours, had our great-grandparents stayed in Russia, we could just as easily have been the Russian guests in their American home. *We* could have been the family of strangers struggling with a new language in a new land.

The Torah is right. What a family does has *consequences* for three, four generations down the road. Yes, collectively, in a small family or a large community, what one person does influences all. And one generation's choices can have consequences for the next—consequences not punishments.

But what about this punishing God, who insists that we do right and is prepared to punish wrong? What about that second question?

The smallest part of me believes in this, literally, that God watches over us, caring and chastising. But in my more rational moments—this means most days under most circumstances—I have trouble accepting the idea that God is omnipotent, omnipresent, omniscient and benevolent. I know that sometimes I will exclaim, "Thank God!" when I get good news from the doctor or the Internal Revenue Service. I will answer a friend's sneeze with a, "God Bless You!" And I will blurt out "Please God!" while running across the airport terminal to catch that flight.

But what about those prayers that ask God to do something, what we call prayers of petition, prayers that said, "I beg you, God! I desperately need your help! God, are you there for me?"

Two thousand years ago, the rabbis of the Mishna saw righteous people pray for rain and the sky remain clear. They saw innocent people pray for health, only to fall ill. Some rabbis thought God just answers the prayers of the righteous. Others said you will hear from God eventually, perhaps in an afterlife. Still others gave us different advice.

Two thousand years ago, our Mishna taught us the following:

> *Crying for what is past is a vain prayer. For instance, if his wife is pregnant and he says, "May it be Your will that my wife*

> *bears a male," this is a vain prayer. If he is walking along and hears wailing in the city and he says, "May it be Your will that it is not coming from my house," this is a vain prayer.*
> (*Mishna Berachot* 9.31)

Two thousand years ago the rabbis gave us this sound advice. God will not change the sex of a fetus. God will not relocate a catastrophe. God will not change the Laws of Nature to suit you, regardless of how hard you pray. So don't pray for God to put a letter from Publisher's Clearing House into your home mailbox. And there is nothing to gain from bursting out, "Dear God! Please give me an "A" just as the teacher is returning the exam. It's not some recent, radical idea. Its what our rabbis taught twenty centuries years ago.

Five hundred years later, the rabbis wondered, "What if a potential crook gets down on the knees and begs, "Dear God, let me be successful tomorrow when I rob that bank?"

> *Rabbi Huna bar Isaac said, "This is a prayer that one does not offer, to steal or perform a sin or do something evil and unsuitable." (Midrash Tehillim*, Buber 176-7)

And will God change people's feelings or actions?

> *Raba once heard a man praying, "Let her be my wife." Raba said to him, "Do not pray this way. If she is the right one for you, she will not leave you. And if not, won't you lose your faith in God?" (Talmud Moed Katan* 18b)

The loss of faith in God! Is God nothing more than a knee-jerk to prayer, an emotional prop for the fainthearted or a myth to shore up the weak-spirited? Is that all God is, our mumbling a few meditations from a book and getting an immediate blessing? Is God some cosmic twenty-four hour phone operator I reach by dialing a liturgical 800 number? Can I call in an order for a world designed exactly to my idiosyncratic specifications? And can I have it delivered next day by Divine overnight mail?

God does not answer the phone when we pray. Some disagree, but I believe God will not change the laws of nature for me or for you. No matter how good a person I am, my prayers will not get God to stop a mugger's bullet mid-air, or halt the flow of the Hudson River. God does not dole out handouts for our goodness or chastise us for our misbehavior.

So the next question is, "If God does not send us stuffed animals, then, pray tell, just what does God do?"

God's Sabbath
The Existential Epic
More Than Just a Day of Rest

"Dennis, always walk tall," said my Grampa on our one-block stroll to the synagogue for the Sabbath morning service. It was one of my occasional overnight visits to my grandparents that included a full Sabbath, an overnight from Friday to Saturday. "Always walk tall, especially today, because today is 'Sahturday.'" Grampa was born in America, but this day was so important that he let creep something of his background into his unaccented native English, giving "Saturday" a little of the Yiddish of "Shabbes."

We reached the synagogue that mild, early spring morning, and I imagined my Grampa on his workday walking several more blocks to the elevated train, the New Lots Line, that would carry him from Brooklyn to the Manhattan office where he did clerical work. I pictured him climbing the four flights of stairs at the station, walking tall with each measured step. But today was "Sahturday" and instead of walking through the turnstile at the elevated he walked into the synagogue with me.

A handful of men sat around the small sanctuary waiting for the service to begin, sharing a light banter with the ease of the New York Yankees passing a baseball around the infield. Their relaxed chatter spoke their confidence that the service would start—sooner or later. The Rabbi sat alone in the front, beside the ark, gazing at the ceiling and smiling to the air, lost in some playful, perhaps prayerful reverie. He did not notice us enter. But Mr. Smith did. He was the *gabbai* and *shammes*, service organizer, leader, and sexton rolled into one, an otherwise semi-retired man like my grandfather. His face clearly revealed a sense of urgency as, with furrowed forehead, he stomped out the door we had just entered.

I remembered Mr. Smith from my earlier visits to this synagogue. Mr. Smith was at shul seven days a week, for morning, afternoon, and evening services. He knew the entire building—which key worked which lock or where to find extra light bulbs. He knew all the people—who receives a particular pulpit honor, who hadn't paid his dues. He knew baseball and he knew Jewish law—and Mr. Smith knew well enough that while nine baseball players are enough to play ball, he needed a quorum of ten males over age thirteen to begin the service. According to my count, my grandfather brought the total to nine, that I, age eleven, was too young to be considered an adult, and it fell to Mr. Smith to rummage up a tenth. While the other eight men chatted as they waited, Mr. Smith set out to scout the street. Within a few minutes Mr. Smith returned to the sanctuary, his brow of consternation and determined stomp having yielded to the grin and swagger of victory. His catch followed close behind—a red faced young teen, dressed in jeans and a T-shirt who I suppose had been shortstopped on his way to play in a ball game. A few whispers and chuckles followed the teen down the aisle. I imagine that the following Saturday morning, he took a different route to the ball field.

Mr. Smith strutted up to the reader's desk in the front of the chapel, and facing the ark with his back to the congregation as was the custom, placed a hand on each side of the podium. Now braced for the start of the service, he opened his Hebrew chant, extending the pronunciation of the first syllable of the first word of the first prayer in a deep and lingering warm bass that yielded to a smooth, fast, and comfortable read through the rest of the paragraph and the service. This voice was worn and polished smooth by days and years of reciting those same prayers. Sometimes when I pray I still hear his voice, a voice that could part the gates of the heavens if not out of authority and stamina then out of hours of love and practice. And that voice did rouse the daydreaming rabbi who sat up in his chair with the first chanted word.

My favorite ritual took place three hours later, after the conclusion of the Saturday morning service. It was the kiddish—a couple of brief prayers followed by food and some more small talk. Mr. Smith took charge of this affair as well, asking two men to accompany him to the tiny kitchen in the back. The two returned ahead of Mr. Smith, carrying the *hallah*, braided bread, the sweet red wine, pickled herring, crackers and paper goods. Mr. Smith followed, bearing a "bottle schnapps"—this week's selection, "J&B"—and a smile even broader and swagger even wider than when he returned with the tenth member of the quorum.

"What's your hurry, Mr. Smith?"
"Hurry? What kept him so long?"
"He must have sipped some back there."

The others took care of the food while Mr. Smith, himself, carefully counted and laid out paper shot cups and filled each one.

"A little more in this one, Mr. Smith!"
"Are you saving the rest for yourself?"
"How else would he get his voice so deep?"

THE TEN COMMANDMENTS

They blessed the bread and the wine. Then they passed out cups of the "Schnapps," even giving one, with a fingernail's contents, to me. The color and smell said, "Lestoil." I tugged at my Grampa's sleeve and he poured me an exchange of another thimble's worth of Maneschewitz sweet red Concord wine. This new cup said "Cheracol" cough syrup.

Now Grampa and Grandma never drank at home. They did keep several unopened bottles of liquor on the shelf, bottles they received as gifts from a work associate of my grandfather's or from some distant relative ignorant of my grandparents' habits. My grandparents saved the liquor to give to the building superintendent or handymen as a "Thank you" for unstopping a sink drip or hanging a light fixture. On the rare occasion when my grandfather did have a drink, at a family wedding, for instance, his face immediately turned a bright red, just as it did as we left the synagogue. And by the time we returned to the apartment that warming April sunny noon, his face looked like he had just walked a mile in below zero wind-chill.

My Grandma saw him as soon as we got back to the apartment. The previous weeks' chilly weather must have smartly masked his Saturday, post-service indulgence well enough. There was a different cold wind today.

His real name was "Nathan" but when my Grandma was angry it became "Natie" as her voice flew up to a high pitch that rang in my ear as an interesting counterpoint to Mr. Smith's deep tone at the other end of the audible spectrum. "Look at your face! You drank that whiskey again! Natie, look at you!"

Grampa stood still and said nothing. I could not tell if he was blushing in embarrassment or red in anger, his face a bright red from the schnapps.

"Did you have any of that whiskey, Dennis?" She looked at him while she asked me.

GOD'S SABBATH: THE EXISTENTIAL EPIC

"No, I didn't drink any whiskey, Granma." To tell the *whole* truth, that Mr. Smith gave me some that I chose not to drink would probably have led to a divorce.

She stared at him for a moment longer before returning to her usual tone of voice. "Your lunch is ready."

Any other day of the week, she would have thrown him out of the apartment. But today was "Sahturday," and on Shabbes you make an exception.

In my childhood, I knew "Shabbes" as a day of prohibition, a day of "no"—a day of no shopping, no money, no writing, and no television. But I also remember the Sabbath as a day of freedom, especially for an adult like my Grampa. For him the Sabbath was a day of liberation from the rush hour grind, a day of freedom from climbing the stairs of the elevated train. The Sabbath was a time for family, together, spared the pressures of work and school. It was a day to sip a schnapps forbidden the other days of the week. And the Sabbath was something even more.

The older gentlemen of the corner synagogue of my youth were not affluent men. American-born or longtime immigrants, a tailor, a shoemaker, a cab driver or a clerk, they held no high titles or professional positions and were of modest means, having gone to work directly out of high school, if not grade school, passing the next four or five decades at the same job, following a boss's or customer's simple instructions in exchange for enough to live on, and maybe a few extra dollars to salt away to supplement social security. Work offered no opportunity for advancement, nor any freedom to be creative or personally expressive. Work meant doing what you had to do to pay for what you needed to have. As the men were not bosses at work, they were certainly not bosses at home. What to eat and when, what to watch on TV, the furniture, carpeting and drapes, even the choice of shirt and socks—wives made all the important decisions, even to the "if" and "when" of having a "schnapps." The Mr. Smiths, then, had no authority at work, at home, in life—until it came to the life of the synagogue, the arena of the holy, the only domain that *really* mattered.

At the synagogue, on the Sabbath, the Mr. Smiths saw themselves in a different light, a Divine light. On the Sabbath, they stood directly before God as proud members of the people of Israel, guardians of the Ten Commandments and all the sacred traditions of Judaism. The rest of the world went to work or went shopping on "Shabbes." On Saturday, when non-Jews watched television and rode on busses or in cars and played baseball, when Jewish wives at home made lunch for the Jewish men at prayer, *we* were the keepers of the four-thousand-year-old sacred pact with God. We chanted the same prayers our ancestors chanted years ago in Europe, and we honored the Torah itself, reading from it, blessing it, even kissing it. Let other people have better jobs, more money and better homes. Let the wives manage the homes. And if it meant stealing the baseball team's ninth player to provide the tenth to fill out our quorum for the Sabbath morning service, let the coach scrounge for that last outfielder, not us! In the synagogue, on the Sabbath, Mr. Smith had all a Jew ever needed—freedom, responsibility, and the opportunity to "walk tall."

The culmination of the Ten Commandments is the Sabbath, a day that occupies a critical position in Jewish law and practice. From before sunrise Friday and until after sunset on Saturday, thirty-nine categories of forbidden labor are proscribed—movement beyond one's residence is limited, nothing carried from one's home out to the street and reverse, no fires are to

GOD'S SABBATH: THE EXISTENTIAL EPIC

be kindled, no writing, cutting, no tying or untying knots and more. The Jew is to be occupied with prayer, study, and meditation, delight with food, wine, song, family, and marital sex, all paying homage to the Sabbath as a reminder of both the creation and the exodus. According to legend, this culmination of the week offers a foretaste of the Messianic Era, a preview of a time of universal peace and harmony—and even more.

The Sabbath is more than a day of rest, more just a day of freedom from having to climb four flights to the elevated, even more than the opportunity to steal an otherwise forbidden drink. One day of the week sets the model for living all seven, placing the commuting and the hurrying into proper perspective. The Sabbath instructs us how to balance the workweek tensions between time and space, having and being, and the ends and the means. The Sabbath is the heart of the Jewish spiritual-ethical experience and at the heart of the Ten Commandments. It is the Sabbath that allows the weaving together the self, family, community, and God in thought, speech, and action. The Sabbath establishes the human as a spiritual being.

If we consider the Torah as one book and its story as an epic narrative story—many little stories artfully woven into one big one—we can identify central themes that carry all the way through the book. One powerful theme—motif or metaphor— is the image of the land, the transition from the cursed earth of Eden to the Promised Land of Canaan via the Ten Commandments.

The "Existential Epic" begins with the story of the creation. With God's few spoken words, an empty darkness explodes into an array of light and life, foliage, animals and human beings, all in the course of six days. As the sun sets on the completed work of creation, God declares the seventh day a Sabbath, a day of cessation of the labor, and calls man and woman to imitate God, to labor for six days and rest every seventh day. But one tragic misdeed in Eden almost undoes the entire glory of creation. Adam and Eve eat the forbidden fruit.

For the snake that duped Eve into touching then tasting the banned fruit, God declares:

> *More cursed shall you be than all the cattle and all the wild beasts. On your belly shall you crawl and dirt shall you eat all the days of your life. I will put enmity between you and the woman, and between your offspring and hers. They shall strike at your head and you shall strike at their heel* (Gen 3:14-5).

For Eve, who eats and transgresses and then offers the forbidden fruit to Adam, God promises:

> *You will suffer miserably in pregnancy. In pain shall you bear children. You will long for your husband, and he shall dominate you* (Gen 3:16).

And God swears to Adam:

> *Cursed be the ground because of you. In misery shall you eat it all the days of your life. Thorns and thistles shall it sprout for you. But your food shall be the grass of the field. By the sweat of your brow shall you eat bread until you return to the ground for from it you were taken. For dust you are and to dust shall you return* (Gen 3:17-9).

All human relationships are cursed because of the transgression—the relationships between people and the earth, people and animal life, man and woman, parent and child, people and their labor, intention and result, and life and death. After Eden, we are all strangers to ourselves, to each other, and to God.

The fertility curse as punishment sets a dismal script for Adam and Eve, for the rest of the Torah, for the entire story of human history, even until today. All of our relationships are now contaminated—the earth, our labor upon it, the relationships between man and woman, and between the woman and her offspring. Even today, in every relationship still, is the tinge of the curse of Eden.

The enmity between the woman and the snake, and later on between her offspring and the snake, symbolize the alienation between people and nature. The challenge of adapting to the seasons—cold and hot, dry and rainy—and the threats of the extremes of nature—blizzards, floods, earthquakes, tornado, hurricanes, pollution, the ruination of our environment—all undo us as they eat away at our well being. We race to cure dread diseases as smallpox or polio until illness reemerges in new forms such as E. coli, ebola, and AIDS. Our bodies are strangers to us. The curse of Eden reminds us that we are strangers on our planet earth.

In the economic challenges we face, the estrangement between farmer and earth is a metaphor for the uneasiness many feel as they attempt to earn a living. In the modern era, downsizing and layoffs seem to be America's most important products. The worker of pre-computer era training in the electronic workplace is the square peg in the round hole, the transistor in place of the microchip, the horse where a car or space shuttle is needed. The metaphor of the cursed earth speaks of the malaise that fills so many trying to earn a living. We are strangers to our earth and our work.

The fall from Eden is a metaphor for another estrangement, one between woman and man. The first couple is not at peace when alone; they find no complete satisfaction with one another either. She suffers from a deep longing for the husband and the painful consequences in pregnancy and delivery once she obtains him. Their embarrassment over their nakedness, the disgrace they feel over the way they look to themselves and each other tells us they are ashamed of themselves, the appetite and curiosity that released their bare instincts and actions, who they are and what they have done. They cannot change the fundamental problems; all they can do is try to hide from their nakedness and guilt. After Eden, we still struggle with gender issues as sexual discrimination and harassment, gender bias, and a glass ceiling. Men and women—we are strangers to ourselves and to each other.

The curse of Eden is substantially a discrepancy between intention and outcome, between what we want and what we get, between hopes and reality. We expect our plantings to yield wheat; but thorns and thistles grow in their stead. The woman seeks the man to satisfy her needs; she also experiences pain and domination. She cannot live without him and does not want to be with him. The curse of Eden is the tragic metaphor for the human condition. And the curse intensifies as we leave Eden and move through subsequent stories of Genesis.

The pain of birth extends itself through the story of the first brothers. After the fall, Eve and Adam bear two sons, Cain, the elder a farmer, and Abel, the younger, the shepherd. The brothers present offerings to God, Cain's of routine quality from the harvest, and Abel's, from the choice of the flocks. God accepts Abel's but rejects Cain's as inferior. Cain, cultivator of the cursed earth, cannot responsibly control his angry reaction to the conditions of his life—that God's favor is not guaranteed, that we cannot expect to reap what we hope to harvest. Cain spills his brother's blood into the mouth of that cursed earth, a cursed land that Cain wanders the rest of his life. No place on earth is Cain's home. The grief and estrangement of the first parents fills the land.

Because of continuing human misconduct, the moral status of the earth deteriorates even further, from "curse" to "corruption." By Noah's time, our sins further poison the earth we walk on. A great flood can wash clean the land—for a while. Noah's family, the only humans righteous enough to be spared death in the flood, remain the final hope. In following chapters, Babel's citizens strive to make a name for themselves, to achieve distinction by building a tower reaching into the heavens. But God confounds their language, breaks them apart into different nations and scatters them across the face of the surface of the soiled land. Only as nomads do we finally find some measure of security. We wander the land, living nowhere for any length of time. And it is in the wilderness that Abraham and Sarah covenant with God, promising them a land flowing with milk and honey, countless offspring, as many as the stars—in sum, the hope of Eden's fertility curse overturned.

But, as God also promised, "the land withholds its strength." Times of drought and famine see Sarah, Abraham, and later their descendants, go down to Egypt, where we flirt with overpowering the fertility curse of Eden—we find food in Egypt and we bear many children. But even there we are not really free from the shadow of Eden. In fact, the curse culminates in Egypt. We may have enough to eat, but our labor becomes enslavement—the ultimate in "dead-end work." And Pharaoh murders our children, drowning them in the Nile, adding more agony to the pain of birth post-Eden. We are the ultimate stranger made into the ultimate slave and the fertility curse of Eden is fulfilled. In slavery, work has no goal, no end. There is no feeling of accomplishment once the job is over. And pregnancy, too, is a labor without a meaningful product when our children are cast into the river to drown. Our covenant promised that we would grow to be as numerous as the stars, so plentiful, like the grains of desert sand that we could not be counted. Now we face slavery, infanticide, and extinction. The horrible curse culminates in Egypt and there seems to be no hope.

The old men of the synagogue may have found work punishing and marriage unfulfilling—thankfully a milder condition of life than Adam and Eve knew after the Fall or we encountered in Egypt, but an echo of Eden just the same. And Eden's curse resonates today. Some species can no longer "strike" at our "heel;" we have struck them down first. Yes, we cultivate wheat instead of weeds, drive tractors instead of oxen, calculate not by hand but electronically—at the price of fouling the land, air, and water. We have responded to the curse by standing up to nature, by punishing it, by striking back at it, as is if the earth, sky, and sea are responsible for our plight.

The prominence and politicization of biomedical issues is another example of our failure to integrate our wants and our realities, the mind and the body, life and mortality. The end-of-life dilemmas (such as assisted suicide) and birth issues (such as abortion) are complicated by economic realities—managed care and political visions and machinations. The angry public discourse is a symptom of a deeper problem—the shadow over the pain of birth and the return to dust at death still live in an only slightly veiled and concealed version of the Eden curse.

Yet the Bible as existential epic shows the way to transform Eden's curse into Canaan's promise; a land that sprouts thorns and thistles can flow with milk and honey. The story of our enslavement and our redemption, the Covenant and the Ten Commandments open the way to make a parched earth into a land of blessing and plenty.

Where the story of the Fall begins with a woman's "Yes," the story of our redemption begins when the women answer, "No!" Shifrah and Puah, the midwives who in Egypt, agents for our childbirth, also became agents for the spiritual rebirth and freedom of the nation. Charged with destroying Hebrew boys in their first moments of life, the two strong, humble midwives stand before a mighty world ruler, Pharaoh, and present a concocted story—the Hebrew women give birth and immediately bounce back to life with vigor, offering no opportunity for implementing Pharaoh's strategy of infanticide. After the Fall, severe birth pains become the woman's curse. As the story of our salvation opens, these two resourceful and brave women transcend the curse of fertility, setting the stage for the woman's second deft maneuver on the path to freedom.

The Bible's curse pivots to blessing on the midwives' strength and nobility. After Pharaoh utters his next decree, to cast the baby boys into the Nile River, one boy, Moses, survives. Moses' sister, Miriam, places her newborn brother into a basket and hides him in the reeds along the Nile River. As Miriam watches, Pharaoh's daughter discovers Moses there and takes him to the royal palace to raise him as her own, where, thanks to the ingenuity of women, Moses grows to become God's primary agent in breaking the chains of our bondage. The women of Israel defy the fertility curse to facilitate Israel's redemption from Pharaoh and the establishment of the Covenant of the Ten Commandments. And the essence of this existential epic is the transformation of curse into blessing through the Ten Commandments.

It is the Covenant of the Ten Commandments that opens the possibility for redemption. The Ten Commandments represent the utopian harmony of thought, speech and action, and an integration of the self, the family, the community and God. Now as we begin to consider the theology of the Ten Commandments, we will see addressed the priority of time over space, being over having and the continuity of the ends and the means. And we find this climax of the Ten Commandments in the Fourth Commandment, in the Sabbath and in its extensions, the sabbatical and Jubilee years, all in the number "seven."

The seven days from one Sabbath to the next, the seven weeks from Passover and the redemption to Shavuot and the revelation, the seven years from the Bible's sabbatical year to the next and the seven sets of seven years until the Bible's Jubilee year are the Ten Commandments' prescription for turning a cursed earth into a promised land.

With the exodus from Egypt, we reinstitute the Sabbath's halt of work; we take one day in seven as a day of cessation from labor. The Ten Commandments begins its description of the Sabbath by telling us:

> *Six days shall you labor and do all your work. But the seventh day is a Sabbath for Adonai, your God. You shall not do any work. You, your son and daughter, your male and female servant, or your animals, or the stranger in your community.*

Later (Exod 23:12), we find

> *On the seventh day you shall cease from labor, in order that your ox and your ass may rest, and that your worker and stranger may be refreshed. One day in seven toil abates; all find freedom from labor, rest and refreshment.*

In Bible times, six days a week, artisans transformed natural products into commercial ones, merchants traveled and bartered, farmers planted and harvested. On the Sabbath all those workweek activities and more—gathering food, travel, and kindling fire—were prohibited. In later Temple and rabbinic times, the sages described thirty-nine forms of labor prohibited on the Sabbath—no cutting, no writing, no harvesting, for example. Today, we can see the Sabbath as more than a day to say, "No!" to work, but as a day to say, "Yes!" to life. Today, the Sabbath can still sweep away the curse of Eden and offer the promise of Canaan. Like my Grandfather, Mr. Smith, and all of us in synagogue that Saturday morning, on the Sabbath, we become God's cohorts redeeming ourselves from the curse of Eden to share in the Covenant of the Ten Commandments.

The Sabbath
Time and Space

It was an uneventful three-hour drive from home into Manhattan for a day of sightseeing with the family. I dropped everyone off at the museum and took the car to the nearest garage and checked the posted parking rates.

"Twenty-three dollars just to park a car for an afternoon!" I thought to myself. "I'll look for a space all day before I pay that much!"

I began the hunt, taking the slow weave through the busy neighborhood streets. There was the lure and disappointment of the empty space beside a fire hydrant and the squeeze past double-parked cars whose drivers shared my feelings about garage rates. I circled once and I circled again, and I began to lose patience. "It's costing me more in gas that it would to park," I said to myself. I began to wonder how much more *time* I'd be willing to spend in order to find a *space*.

Most days we give priority to space over time. A builder makes time to transform space—empty lots—into homes or offices. A decorator devotes time to beautify space—filling a bare room with furniture or perking up a blank wall. And anyone who works to pay the rent puts in time to pay for the space called "home." During the workweek, time serves space. And most of the time there is nothing wrong with our actions that say space is more important than time. Even our Fourth Commandment proclaims: Six days shall you labor and do all your work. But come Friday eve, we put aside the work of the week.

When I was a child we kept a small Jewish calendar on our kitchen wall. All our important appointments—doctor visits, birthdays, social commitments—fit onto those tiny calendar pages. But now, a fat appointment book does not have enough space to hold all that I have to do in a day at work. And when I add family obligations, the week is so full that only a computerized schedule would be of much help. It seems relatively easy to control space, relatively easy to keep the living room clear of clutter or get the car from the house to the supermarket. When winter comes, we turn up the heat and warm up our space, but to turn up time in winter and make it summer again, there we have a problem. To move my car across space, from home to the office, is usually not an issue. But, when I am late, the stress that comes from trying to do the trip in record time is the result of Eden's curse. And it is the Sabbath that chastises us to remember, "You may triumph in space, but you are subservient to time."

In his remarkable little book called, *The Sabbath* (*Farrar, Straus, and Giroux, 1951*), the late Rabbi Abraham Heschel looks at the Sabbath commandments and offers us some sound advice toward balancing the demands and conflicts of time and space.

One would think that Judaism is a religion of space. After all, we say that our synagogues are holy spaces, that God dwells in our synagogue sanctuaries. And what about the holy land of Israel, Jerusalem, and above all, the remains of the great, ancient Temple, the Western Wall? And when the Ten Commandments tell us that

THE SABBATH: TIME AND SPACE

Six days shall you labor and do all your work,

the Torah wants us to know that the process and products of labor, the things we make, things of space are at the heart of the tradition. Yes, the Ten Commandments want us to know that things of space—menorahs, Torah scrolls, and ritual ornaments—are what God wants.

But look back to the first story of the first space, the story of the creation of the universe, the products of God's labor. One would think that of all the spaces God set out, God would pick one place and declare that one area a holy space, as if God would point to a particular spot and say, "This one is mine." But, when God initially reflects on the work of creation, looking over the seas and the dry land, the plants, the trees and their fruits,

God saw that this was good (Gen 1:12).

Later on in the world's first week, when God perused the sky, the sun and the moon, the swarms of living creatures in the sky and in the sea and all the beasts of the land

God saw that this was good and God blessed them (Gen 1:21).

After the first six days, God says the products of labor, the creations of space are, "good," if not outright "blessed." But when it comes to the creation of time,

And God blessed the seventh day and declared it holy, because on it God ceased from all the work of creation which God had done (Gen 2:3).

Space is just "good" and people are "blessed," but time is "holy." Writes Rabbi Heschel:

> Now what was the first holy object in the history of the world? Was it a mountain? Was it an altar? . . . The mythical mind would expect that, after heaven and earth have been established, God would create a holy place—a holy mountain or holy spring—whereupon a sanctuary is to

be established. Yet it seems to the Bible it is the holiness in time, the Sabbath, which comes first." (9)

Things of "space" are on the continuum of "good" to "blessed." But when we come to "time," we enter a different domain altogether, the realm of the "holy," the sacred, spiritually elevated, set apart from the commonplace. Yes, there may well be something holy about space, but the holiness of time comes first.

There is another example of the priority of time in the story of the Tent of Meeting. The Tent of Meeting, also known as the Tabernacle, was at the center of Israel's ritual life those forty years of wandering through the Sinai wilderness. While the portable sanctuary belonged to "the people" for worship, the actual daily use of the Tent and its contents—the altar, the candelabrum, the Ark of the Covenant and all the other utensils of the sacrificial rituals—was strictly limited to particular individuals at particular times. The Torah rigidly regulated the when and how of the Tent of Meeting, from peace offerings to sin offerings, from animal offerings to grain offerings. And the Ark of the Covenant, containing the Ten Commandments, rested in the Holy of Holies, the interior and most sacred portion of the Tent of Meeting; a violation of the rules of entry of the Holy of Holies was punishable by death. This was holy space, as holy as space ever gets.

The members of Israel's tribe of Levi were responsible for the daily care of the Tent of Meeting and its sacred vessels. Each time the people of Israel broke camp, the members of the tribe of Levi dismantled the Tent, prepared the Tent and its contents for the journey, and carried it all for the duration of the trip. When the people stopped to make camp, the Levites set up the Tent of Meeting for the resumption of worship rituals.

THE SABBATH: TIME AND SPACE

The Levites, half custodians, half moving company, worked under the careful eye of the Priests, Aaron and his descendants, who bore the ultimate responsibility for conducting Israel's worship. Even the Priests had to follow all of the Torah's strict requirements. Carelessness within the Tent of Meeting could cost a priest's life, as it sometimes did. So one might ask, "How could holy time be more sacred?"

When the Tent occupied a particular site, the "footprint" of the Tent was holy ground. But once the Levites dismantled the Tent of Meeting and moved it on, the way the Bible explains it, the holiness went with the Tent. Imagine having been there, in the Sinai wilderness after the Levites packed up and carried off the last pieces of the Tent of Meeting. Imagine walking around the campsite where the Tent of Meeting had just stood. All we would have found was an empty place, just another camel stop. The holiness lasted only as long as the Tent was there. And had we gotten a jump on our Levite porters and reached the new campsite before they did, we would have found nothing special. The place had no sacred status before the Tent arrived and had none once the Tent left.

Now look at the spaces of the Passover story. No one can show us the burning bush where Moses first met God and God appointed Moses redeemer. No one can find the spot where the Sea of Reeds parted nor can anyone point to where Moses died and was buried. And try to find the real Mount Sinai where Moses received the Ten Commandments. Moses left no sign or engraved plaque to mark the spot. Oh, we point to the highest peak in the Sinai Peninsula, we look at the map and say, "We think this was it." And when I visited the Sinai desert we climbed it—or at least I think I did. You see, no one can conclusively prove that I got to the top of the right one. Yes, the Torah deals with the holiness of space. It goes on for chapters about the land of Israel and the Tent of Meeting and *where*. But the Torah is more concerned with *what* we do and *when*. True holiness is more a matter of time than space. And we see this truth today.

As a Rabbi, from time to time I have the privilege of conducting a wedding ceremony. After the ceremony is over, I will usually return to the *huppa* or marriage canopy and collect my papers. As I get my things in order, I might I pause to think about what just happened in that space that is now empty and quiet, that same space that just a few moments earlier was filled with the holiness of people—their laughter, their words, their tears, and their song. And now that the people are gone, the holiness has gone as well. Now the place is empty and very ordinary.

There is nothing "wrong" with the space that held the ceremony. That space, where we had the ceremony, was "good," perhaps "very good." But time, what really held the ceremony, that moment in time is sacred. Let them change the space, let them empty the chapel of people, dismantle the marriage canopy and sweep the floor. The space has no memory of the event. Once the people are gone, the event is gone from the space; the space was filled with holiness only as long as the people filled the room. What happened lives on in the minds of the people that were there. Time and memory last forever. And it is not just in the Bible and at weddings that we see the holiness of holy time.

We took our kids to see the circus when it came to town. The circus was in a tent—one quite unlike the Bible's Tent of Meeting. Nevertheless, we laughed together, as a family, at the clowns in our tent, the jugglers, and all the other acts. The looks on the kid's faces alone were worth the price of admission.

THE SABBATH: TIME AND SPACE

A few days after the circus left, I stopped by the lot where the show had taken place. The tent was gone—all I saw of it were the holes in the ground where they drove in the stakes. The cars in the parking area were gone—only tire marks in the grass remained. Once the circus moved, all the noise and excitement went with it. Where I once had to pay to enter, I was able to stand for free. But I know that the memory of that show will be with our children for the a long time. Whenever someone mentions a circus, they will remember the experience we shared as a family. The point is that the show could have been anywhere, across the town or across the state. What did matter was the time. For an evening, we shut out the world to enjoy fantasy and laughter. Together as a family, we put aside doctor appointments and car pooling for a moment in time.

Taking time over space is really a very simple thing to do. In fact, we do it instinctively. I consider my home important; the space my family and I occupy is a critical part of my life. But I am more concerned about the quality of time, the home life I enjoy once I close my front door—a loving family can live just about anywhere. And what about my home as a child? My memories are not as much memories of space—the physical neighborhood—as much as they are memories of time—what we did, the games my cousins and I played on the stoop, the Passover Seder around the family table. What's more, I went back to the old neighborhood not long ago and it was so drastically changed that I felt as if I was in a different place. What's more important, a birthplace or a birthday? We react to the mention of a birthplace, say Brooklyn, with a cheer. But we go even further when a birthday comes around, and we celebrate that with a party! Things of space are only temporary, they change, they become different. But memories are of time and time is eternal; what happens in time always stays the same. Yes, space can be special, even holy. But when it comes to the creation of the universe, when it comes to the Tent of Meeting and when it comes to me and to you, time is holier than space. And it seems that when we race against time, time will always win.

When I think back to the old men of the Brooklyn synagogue, I now realize they knew all of this as well, although they never said it to me in words. If it came to a question of space, they could have said those prayers anywhere. When it came to time, they had to do it on the Sabbath. And their prayers, said at the right time, transcended all borders of space and all limits of time. So Judaism is a portable religion. Its important moments, more concerned with "when" than with "where," offer the opportunity to overcome the memory of Eden and the harder conditions of life.

Rabbi Heschel also points out that the Judaism of the Bible, is more concerned with time than with space, more with history than with geography, more with the seasons and their festivals than with regions of the land of Israel and their topography. It is not as much a matter of the architecture of space as it is a matter of the architecture of time.

The new moon and the full moon, day and night, darkness and light, these are at the heart of the biblical religious experience. When Moses led us from slavery to freedom, that incident became the event of time at the core of the story of the festival of Passover. When Moses brought us the Ten Commandments, that moment became the basis for the festival of Shavuot. And the origins of the festival of Sukkot rests in "when" we wandered the Sinai wilderness. We build our holy days around events of time, especially the Sabbath.

The old men of the synagogue knew that the Sabbath, created last, comes first. During the week, we are subjugated to time. We control space when we build

THE SABBATH: TIME AND SPACE

and shape, place numbers on balance sheets, try out the fit of a pair of new shoes and send packages across town and across the world. But on the Sabbath, we make an acknowledgement—as adept as we are with things of space, as much as we fight to stick to the schedule and triumph over time, we defeat space, but time ultimately wins. From the time of birth to the time of death, from the school schedule to the work schedule, we are subordinate to time and its deadlines.

> All week long we are called upon to sanctify life through employing things of space. On the Sabbath, it is given us to share in the holiness that is in the heart of time. (101)

And paradoxically, when we defer to our shortcomings we overcome them.

After Eden, it appears time will always win; death is triumphant, final, and permanent. It will always come. But the Ten Commandments open the possibility that we can overcome time. As long as our thoughts, speech and actions are in keeping with the Ten Commandments and the Bible, we can sweep aside the punishment and become eternal partners in the timeless and universal Covenant our Decalogue represents. But I am getting ahead of myself.

For now, we see that the Sabbath is more than a day to say "No," more than a day of rest or a day of freedom from work or freedom to sneak a drink. Where the weekday offers the opportunity to fill our space with things, the Sabbath offers the opportunity to yield to time and to transcend it. My grandfather and the other men of the synagogue had community—a lifelong and beyond connection, a godlike connection with people. They had a divine task to perform—worship, the acknowledgement of something higher than themselves. They empowered themselves by fulfilling an ongoing responsibility to a transcendent, historic process. They became the safekeepers of God's Covenant, keeping alive the eternal spiritual link between God and Israel. On the Sabbath, they saw that life was not the things they *had* but the people they *were*—how they ceased work like God and lived the life of the Sabbath.

The Bible warns us that the sins of the ancestors will be inflicted on the children. And when we have fouled the earth, air, and water with the waste of our economic production and other daily activities, later generations do suffer illness and hardship for the misdeeds of generations earlier. Yet the Sabbath offers hope and vision for the space we have since Eden has soiled; it is a day of rest for us, for the fragile earth and for the universe. And when we come to the extension of the Sabbath in the sabbatical and Jubilee years, we will see how the God of time enables the worldly space to regenerate and restore itself to the cleanliness and wholeness we knew before the Fall.

So the Sabbath speaks of a time to be in time. On the Sabbath our Eternal God of time has us be concerned with what happens in time—with the godlike potential in what we do and what we are. In other words, the Sabbath is not a time to have, but a time to be.

God's Sabbath
Having and Being

A law against idolatry made sense long ago when people worshipped idols of carved wood or chiseled stone. To coerce these inanimate Gods to bring rain for crops or make cattle and sheep bear healthy young, the ancients sacrificed children and committed adultery through rituals of temple prostitution. But today, idolatry is dead, and it seems we ought to strike the Second Commandment and replace it or just make do with a list of nine. Child sacrifice and cultic prostitution are no more. And for the most part, the closest any of us come to presenting a burnt offering on an altar happens when we throw a steak onto a grill—and there is no sin in a barbecue. Idolatry is all history—and it seems the commandment against idolatry is obsolete.

Not long ago, the author of the Midrash collection, Akedat Yitzhak, Rabbi Isaac Arama, considered the same question, but came to a different conclusion. He maintains that

> Idolatry as it exists today is quite strong. Many people invest all their thought and effort in achieving wealth and success. These are their mighty gods and upon them do they rely. "If I have made gold my hope, or have called fine gold my shelter; if I rejoiced because

my wealth was great and because my hand has gotten much . . . (Job 31:24-28)

Rabbi Isaac Arama makes a rock solid argument. The Bible's idols are made by people, and when the Bible's people pray to idols, they really pray to the products of their own hands, that is to say, they pray to themselves. And the idolatry of self-worship and self-centeredness is exactly what the Ten Commandments want us to avoid. The Jewish tradition does not want us boasting, "The clothing I wear puts me above other people," or "I have a few more dollars than you so I'm worth more." The Bible would have us learn the words of the prophet Hosea (14:4), that when we say to the work of our human hands, "You are our Gods," we have committed an act of idolatry. In an insightful comment to Hosea's observation, commentator Metsudat David notes

> *The idol is made by the work of our hands. It is not to be taken as divine.*

So we have it. We do not construct God.

Over twenty-five years ago, Erich Fromm, a psychoanalyst and social critic wrote a book called *To Have or to Be?* (Harper & Row, 1976). In it, he argued that there is nothing wrong with having, nothing wrong with having a lovely home, a good car or beautiful children or grandchildren. But every once in a while we ought to deal less with having and more with being.

Most of the time we want to have. In fact, we are so good at having, we tell ourselves we own many things that cannot possibly be ours at all. For instance, I will happily wish you, "Have a good day," without thinking that a day is time and time is not to be had. Time is to be experienced. "I have a cold," I remarked the last time I was sick, but the germs were not mine because if I really had them, I would have quickly gotten rid of them. "I cannot have a problem," writes Erich Fromm "because [a problem] is not a thing that can be owned; [the problem] however, can have me. That is to say, [I have made] myself into a problem." Better to say, "I am troubled . . ." (9) I have a happy marriage? You don't own your husband or hold title to your wife—the relationship does not belong to anybody. "Love is not a thing one can have, but a process, an inner activity . . . I can love, I can be in love, but in loving I have . . . nothing." (10) So we do not have half of what we think we have.

But we are not the first generation to emphasize having at the expense of being. After forty years of wandering through the Sinai wilderness, the people of Israel were about to take possession of the Promised Land. Now the people would eventually occupy the land by tribes—each tribe was assigned to a particular area. As the people of Israel prepared to enter the land, they knew that they would cross the border, first passing through regions assigned to the tribes of Reuben and Gad. And the tribes of Reuben and Gad, so excited were they to settle in their new homes, they presented their idea to their leader, Moses.

> *They approached him and said, "We will build here sheep pens for our flocks and towns for our children"* (Num 32:16)

before going on to help the rest of the people with setting into their own communities.

Now Moses believed in community and he wanted the people of Israel to stick together as one nation. And I am sure he was not happy to hear that two of his tribes wanted to break ranks. But as Rashi observes, when Reuben and Gad spoke to Moses, they mentioned their sheepfolds before their towns. Moses became angry because

> *They paid more attention to their wealth than their sons and daughters because they mentioned their cattle first.*

Moses told them that they had it backwards:

> *Build towns for your children and sheep pens for your flocks* (Num 32:24).

Moses wanted all of Israel to know that people come before possessions. Moses taught us that when we select things of space over action in time, when we choose to have rather than to be, we live under the curse of Eden instead of the promise of Canaan.

We were nomads four thousand years ago, desert wanderers. And writes Erich Fromm

> The desert ... is the place of nomads who own what they need, and what they need are the necessities of life, not possessions . . . [they had a] tendency against all non-functional property . . . (an) unfettered, nonpropertied life . . . (38)

No wonder we wanted an invisible God. In the days before moving vans, when we had to carry with us all we owned, who wanted to trudge through the desert lugging around those heavy graven stone idols? We had a portable religion and carried only what we absolutely needed. An invisible God helped us nomads—kept us away from the idol of having and helped us keep our baggage light.

I took my last lesson in modern idolatry when our family moved from Washington, DC to the Berkshires. We were apartment nomads earlier in our married life. But once we began the settled life of raising three children, we had more than we could handle, much more than the proverbial boxes in the basement that we had not opened during the ten years since we were married.

I began the monumental moving job by preparing our library. I boxed, sealed, and inventoried, and weighed what turned out to be three-quarters of a ton of books in 115 boxes, each box no more than the United Parcel Service regulation seventy pounds. On the day we said goodbye to our boxes, all at once, four dark olive trucks pulled up in front of our home and four drivers in khakis jumped out to clear our garage. Then, a few weeks later, it took four more strong, hardworking movers a ten-hour day to fill to bursting the largest moving van on the road. And as the van pulled away from the curb to travel to our new home four hundred miles away, I remembered that the first Jews did not have it like this. Today, many of us have a good deal more than we can carry by ourselves or transport on the backs of a caravan of camels. And it is not just that we have too much stuff.

I think of Arama's definition of idolatry whenever we measure the worth of people on the basis of what they have. Day in and day out, we may base our estimate of a person's value by the yardstick of the dollar value of a stock portfolio. And we commonly speak of a twenty-five-cent candy bar or a three-quarter of a million-dollar house, long after the deal has been brought to a close. It's not a matter of what it does for me or someone else, how it works, but what I can get for it were I to sell it, only that I want to keep it—the thing is not for sale. Does it make sense to seem more concerned with what we paid than with what we are going to do? When we turn to what we own, we really don't have half of what we think. And of the things that really do belong to us, why we ought to stop making as much of them as we often do.

Now there is nothing wrong with having. Imagine life without the things that the law of this land and Jewish law say "I have." Imagine life without having a bite to eat now and then, without having a roof over our heads, without having a family, without having friends and community. Even the earliest Jews, Abraham and Sarah, had a great deal of wealth, according to our Torah. But, their material possessions were not at the center of their lives. God was at their spiritual core, God, family, and community. For most of the time, it is fine to think of having. But when we speak of living the life of the covenant, we set for ourselves a time to be.

It was a moment of insight in the Bible, when God asked Moses to lead the people of Israel from slavery to freedom.

> Moses said to God, "When I come to the people of Israel and say to them, 'The God of your ancestors has sent me to you,' and they ask me, 'What is this God's name?' what shall I say to them?" God said to Moses, "ehyeh asher ehyeh." "I will be what I will be.'" "I will be," said God (Exod 3:13-4).

Being is God's name. God is not a deity of having, a God of idols, a God of the material. Our God is not in the sun or in the moon, in the trees or in the rain, in animals or in the wind. Our God is one of being, in what we are and in what we do. An idol is a god that just sits there, and takes up space. An idol stands for the status quo. Stagnant, unchanging, each day for the finished idol is the same. But the God of being, the God of time is a changing, becoming God, a God of growth. And when we speak of our God of being, we pledge that we can remove the curse of Eden from life.

So we do not "have" a God the way one would "have" dinner or "have" a new car. And we do not experience God when we collect our things of space. We encounter God's being in moments of time, in the day in and day out of human events and in the course of human history, in routine family life and in the exodus from Egypt, in the birth of a child, in the birth of a nation, in deep reflection, and in heartfelt self-examination. We can experience God in the moment of insight when we call out "Aha!" or when we realize, "Look how I have grown and what I have become, I am different than I once was!" We do not see God in the children we "have," but when we help our children as they step by step learn to be. God is always becoming, says the Torah and so are we. God never stands still, and neither do we. When a friend extends a helping hand to one who is bereaved or when a community organizes itself to take care of one of its own, God is. Eric Fromm taught us that the idol is not becoming, it does not grow because by the time a piece of wood becomes an idol it is already finished. It is a stagnant thing of space. The invisible God, on the other hand, is "a negation of idols, of gods whom one can have" (31) We do not find our God when we find the one who owns the most. We see God in the person who lives doing the most, who achieves as much a possible within the time for living that one is allotted. We do not find God when we are static like the idol. Instead, we see God when a person grows in time.

The invisible God of being is also the God of time. For it is during the time of the Sabbath that the God of being in time can be fully experienced.

> The Shabbat was the fountain of life for the Jews, who scattered, powerless and often despised and persecuted, renewed their pride and dignity when like kings they celebrated the Shabbat. Is the Shabbat nothing but a day of rest? . . . If this were all that it was, the Shabbat would hardly have played the central role . . . it is rest in the sense of the reestablishment of complete harmony between human beings and between them and nature . . . nothing may be destroyed and nothing be built; the Shabbat is a day of truce in the human battle with the world. Even tearing up a blade of grass is looked upon as a breach of this harmony, as is lighting a match. Neither must social change occur. On the Shabbat one lives as if one has nothing, pursuing no aim except being, that is expressing one's essential powers: praying, studying, eating, drinking, singing, making love. (39-40)

For a day, we stop transforming things. The Sabbath is a day to be more, more in touch with family and community, with ourselves and with our God. We are to fill the first six days of the week with our labor, but of the seventh the goal of life is being, not having, creating a day away from the cursed earth, away from making things of space. So my stock market holdings may rise in value or they may fall. I can expand my house or sell it, but with all these transactions of having, I am still the same person with a few dollars more to spend or a few dollars less, with an extra room at home to ramble through or not. As a person, whether I have or not, I am still the same.

In fact, the Ten Commandments are all commandments of being, not having. They tell us not to covet, that what your neighbor has should stay there, that you and I are to leave it *be*. The prohibition of murder teaches us to let others *be*, let them take in the quiet enjoyment of life. "Do not commit adultery" means there is a proper way to *be* in relation to one's spouse. And the commandment not to take false witness—"*Be* truthful."

So this is the life of the Sabbath, a day to be for oneself, a day for the animal to graze freely for itself, a day for all people to pursue their own end and not someone else's, to live in time, to live in being, to transcend space, to transcend our possessions, one day a week to live life not by the business contract, but by a religious covenant. The Sabbath is the one day of the week that sets the paradigm for living all the other days.

10

God's Sabbath
Ends and Means

To take time over space and being over having brings us to the door of redemption. To take the next steps, to fully conquer the curse of Eden today, means we need to go beyond the Sabbath day to the Sabbath year, in fact, to the life of the Sabbath. We look at the sabbatical and Jubilee years, and the concept of a utopian society begins to emerge, a national community that brings all of us to a life of blessing.

In the wilderness of Sinai, God commands us to count six days and declare the seventh day a Sabbath, a day of cessation from labor. Later, when we have settled into the farm life of Canaan, the Torah tells us to count six years and declare every seventh year a sabbatical year for the land. In an agricultural society, the entire economy revolves around the land. People make their homes on the land. The land is where farmers labor and beasts plough, land offers the only real possibility of economic security. For one year, there is no cultivation; whatever grows, will grow—food, thorns, or grass. The land exists, not as a means to a human end but as an end in its own. And for one year, the curse disappears.

Of all the peoples in the Ancient Near East, only Israel kept the sabbatical year. For a full calendar year, the farmer does not plow, harvest, or do any work on the land. And the farmer has no right to what grows this year; it is to be shared with the poor, the widow, the orphan, and the stranger—all of society's landless and powerless. In a world where income, social status, and personal security come from what one owns, in a year that no one really owns the farm, only the penniless are to enjoy the products of the land. It is their sabbatical year off in the ongoing struggle to survive. And the Hebrew bondsman and bondswoman are to be freed in this sabbatical year. The indentured servant, once sold into domestic slavery to honor a debt can now return home, entirely free to be.

This year we recognize that God who created the land is its rightful owner. The earth grows naturally, all by itself, unmanipulated in the battle to force the land to sprout the particular things that serve our human needs. In the sabbatical year, the land does not serve people's ends; it serves itself. And by letting the poor gather what grows freely, God's land redeems the powerless among us the way God redeemed us when we were powerless slaves in Egypt. We use this year to overturn the curse of the land, suspend the vexing earthbound labor and live peacefully on the land, in blessing, with family and community, in contemplation of the God who created us, sustaining the powerless poor with our holding. We release our space and sanctify our time, and turn to our being instead of our having. We live a year when people and the land are an end in themselves, and not a means to someone's end. The sabbatical year is a time when the self, its thought, speech and action, lives in harmony with the family, community and God. For one full year, we turn what was cursed in Eden into a blessing in Canaan.

At the end of seven sets of seven years, after forty-nine years came the Jubilee year, the fiftieth year of liberty for all. Twice in a century, all slaves and indentured servants were let free and returned to their homelands. In the Jubilee year all land sold in the prior forty-nine years returns to the original owners or their descendants. All people, including those who sold themselves into servitude to pay their debt, are now free and can live on their own land which is now returned to them.

Countering the natural human tendency to accumulate wealth, to centralize ownership of the land and the power that flows from that ownership, God declares,

> *The land shall not be sold permanently, for the land is mine* (Lev 25:23).

In a society where God was the rightful owner of all, citizens calculated the price of a land purchase by counting the number of years remaining until the Jubilee. What one sold were annual harvests. In the year immediately after a Jubilee, the land cost more since more crops could be planted and reaped. The years just before a Jubilee, a purchaser took out a short-term lease, with fewer years for growing, fewer years for payment. All this works against social stratification that comes from the concentration of wealth, from the power that comes from "having" that money and ruling over that "space." In an extension of the redeeming power of the Sabbath, the ordinary rules of "having" in "space" yielded to the divinely ordained command to "be" in "time" and encounter the sacred. And taken together, the weekly Sabbath and the years of sabbatical and Jubilee portray a utopian harmony of economic, political, social, ecological, and theological ends and means.

In an economic sense, people are no longer tools of someone else's business, slaving for someone else under Eden's curse. The most important tools of earning—people—for a time, return to *be* people for themselves, not indentured employees of someone else. As God redeemed us from the curse of our labor in Egypt, all indentured workers are now freed from their labor. We who God redeemed from powerlessness are now to imitate God and finish redeeming ourselves along with the next person who faces estrangement.

In a political sense, the power we attain through this ownership ends. One day a week, one year of every seven, people are on a more equal level of power. We coerce no one in thought, speech, or action. For a time, people are free, allowed to be. The political end and the means to that end are one.

In a social sense, people can return to life as private human beings, living for themselves directly in covenant with God. We return from working the land and things of space to living with each other, family, community, and God, being with each other in time. Husband, wife, servant, neighbor—each person is an end in himself or herself. And the poor can gather food as they wish, even on the land of another. All can live on their own, in free relation to one another. God freed Israel from Pharaoh and gave the Ten Commandments to teach that the right to the land and the right to life on the land belong to all.

In an ecological sense, the land lives for itself as well. We do not this year fight with the land under the curse. What grows on it will grow. What animals wish to cross it and eat of it will do so. For one year the land is for itself—not a tool of the farmer, but an object of God's creation. The Sabbath, sabbatical, and Jubilee teach an ecological message that God owns it all, not you and not me. The world is God's—not ours. The land does not belong to us; if anything we belong it. Most every primary school child I talk to can lecture me about the ethics of recycling or the economics and science of composting. These children tell us that the earth will carry on, that they will have a world to live in, only if we recognize that the earth is in our trust, that it can get used up, that our rights to use it are not absolute.

No one can prove that all this really did happen, that we had enough food in store to go one year out of seven without any intentional agricultural production, that we survived off our stores for two years in a row after seven sets of seven. And even if all this did happen, I cannot promise that we will ever again build a society capable of sustaining such institutions. But this is not the point.

The Bible wants to establish an ideal, that we can improve this world, that we can free ourselves of the pharaohs we meet in labor or in society, that we can strive for a world where people can be ends in themselves and not tools for others. Whether it really happened or not, whether this is our actual history or not, the sabbatical cycles establish a religious ideal, founded in the Ten Commandments, the vision of a just society—nomadic, agricultural, industrial, or informational.

One day a week, one year in seven, one year after seven sets of seven, the end and the means are one. The day-in, day-out of Eden, alienation of intention and product, the continual mismatches of our marital, familial, professional, communal, and international relationships are all reconciled on the Sabbath. According to our eternal, universal Covenant, we live under the curse only for six days, six years. On the seventh, we are free.

So the Sabbath is not just a little vacation, another day off of school or work that we use to again marshal our strength for another busy week. Yes, the Sabbath may help us become more efficient in the office but that is a by-product of the Sabbath's goal. The goal is justice, harmony, and equality, a harmony of thought, speech, and action. The intent is to ground our thoughts, words, and deeds in covenantal principle, consistency, and integrity. The goal is the self, family, community, and God, a confluence of man and woman, people and earth, time and space, having and being, a moment when all our ends and all our means are joined into a harmonious whole. The Sabbath is a time to imitate God, to redeem ourselves, the stranger and all others from the curse of Eden and the Pharaohs of today. Yes, there is a clear, workable theology in the Covenant of the Ten Commandments.

There are two versions of the Ten Commandments in the Torah—one in Exodus and one in Deuteronomy. They are substantially the same but there are some differences. The Fourth Commandment, for the Sabbath, holds one of the greater differences.

In exodus we read (with the crucial textual differences in italic)

> *Remember* the Sabbath day to make it holy. Six days shall you labor and do all your work, but the seventh day is a Sabbath for the Eternal, your God. You shall not do any work, you, your son and daughter, your male and female servant, your animals, or the stranger in your community. *Because in six days Adonai made heaven and earth and the sea and all that is in them, and God rested on the seventh day. Therefore, Adonai blessed the seventh day and made it holy.*

The Deuteronomy version reads

> *Observe* the Sabbath day to make it holy. Six days shall you labor and do all your work, but the seventh day is a Sabbath of the Eternal, your God. You shall not do any work, you, your son and daughter, your male and female servant, your animals, or the stranger in your community, so that your male and female slave may rest as you do. *You shall remember that you were a slave in the land of Egypt and the Eternal, your God freed you from there with a mighty hand and an outstretched arm. Therefore,*

the Eternal, your God, has commanded you to observe the Sabbath day (Deut 5:12-15).

The idea leads to the action; Deuteronomy replaces Exodus's milder "Remember" with the stronger "Observe" to tell us that "Thinking is nice, but acting is crucial." But even more critically, where Exodus says that the Sabbath comes from the creation, Deuteronomy finds the source of the Sabbath in the redemption from Egypt, and here we have the essence of the Covenant and the Ten Commandments—our humble, human actions are to imitate God's.

Six days shall you labor and do all your work

describes our six days of creation, parallel to God's in Genesis where

in six days the Eternal made heaven and earth and sea and all that is in them.

For six days, our creative work is the equivalent of God's creative work.

On the Sabbath, according to Exodus, we rest because

God rested on the seventh day.

We imitate God by ceasing work, just the way God did. According to Deuteronomy, we keep the Sabbath because

you were a slave in the land of Egypt and Adonai, your God, freed you from there.

To Deuteronomy, we imitate God by being the Redeemer, helping ourselves and others bask in the redemption the Sabbath offers. By imitating God, resting and redeeming, we fulfill our eternal Covenant and live under the blessing of Canaan, free of the shadow of Eden.

For this is what the conclusion of the Ten Commandments promises, the *blessings and curses* of Leviticus, the grand conclusion of the Decalogue. Immediately after its description of the sabbatical and Jubilee years, the Torah outlines the consequences of keeping—or breaking the Covenant.

> *If you walk by My statutes and keep My commandments and do them*

says God

> *Then I will give you rain in its season so the land can yield its produce and the trees of the field their fruit*

Instead of grasses and thorns, the earth will offer up food—what we need and want—an agricultural bounty and the blessing of plenty that

> *Your threshing shall last until the time of vintage and the vintage shall last until the time of sowing. You shall eat your fill of bread and dwell safely in your land. I will give you peace in the land and you shall lie down at night and none will make you afraid. I will rid the land of evil beasts and the sword will not go through your land . . . For I will look upon you favorably and make you fruitful and multiply you and keep my Covenant with you . . . I will dwell among you . . . I will walk among you and be your God and you shall be my people. I am Adonai, your God, who brought you out of the land of Egypt* (Lev 26:3-13).

The text goes on to describe the illness, famine, war, and loss of our home that will follow if we are not faithful. And the choice is ours.

Our lives imitate God when we live the Covenant—in the ideal society our work and rest are on a level with God's. We wandered the Sinai for forty years until God saw we were ready to live life of the Sabbath on the Promised Land. Once the wandering ended, God let us enter the land and, through the Covenant, God made it possible for us to remove our curse and live in blessing. We are free and we are responsible, shunning the forbidden fruits of life outside the Covenant, living under the blessing of Canaan, wife and husband and child in love, the land offering them its fill, with an overriding harmony among all peoples. This is the Bible's ideal of the life in the ideal society in the Covenant of the Ten Commandments with God.

Perhaps the promised time is not in a place we reach when we have finished some long life journey, nor is the promised time an era that arrives when the moment is right. Perhaps we can reach that time, right now. I can see glimmer of it each day. When my wife rises from bed past midnight to comfort our crying child, when I banter about the warming weather with the supermarket cashier, when the bride and groom standing before me smile as they look at each other in a triumphant silence that says, "Our moment is here," when there is relief on faces at a funeral when the last relative arrives from the airport and the entire family is together, when I fix my child's broken toy, when the kids jump to my "Lets go for a bike ride," or when I hold my daughter up on the deck of the Maid of the Mist at Niagara Falls, both of us drenched by the water spray, despite those flimsy plastic ponchos, when our Temple Sabbath worship connects us to Jews praying around the world, to the old men of the Brooklyn synagogue of my youth and to any Jew who ever prayed, when someone new to Judaism in study of the Torah finds something in that sacred text that all these years I never imagined existed, and when I finally get to look at my wife at 11:00 PM, at the end of a non-stop day, both of us too tired to retell the events of the fourteen hours just past, bracing to prepare ourselves for the next one.

I am not sure that any of these moments bring our world or ourselves closer to the end of time when everything will be healed. But I do know that I can live this dream, this utopian vision, for an hour or an evening, for a moment. I have lived in Canaan, spent a moment in the Promised Land where the blessing won over the curse.

"They told me that my wife belongs here," he said, gesturing left with his left hand, "and that my spirit belongs here," gesturing to the far right with his right hand. "And I just can't get things to go where they belong." This young husband, father to a little boy, a student of a faith far from my own, was spiritually torn apart as he came to me in deep doubt over the lessons of his spiritual discipleship.

His teachers preached of the need to cultivate the spirit by pushing aside people and things. Longings for other persons and material goods are distractions from spiritual truth, to be shunned. His responsibility was a religious discipline of meditative exercises, internal cultivation, with little success, leaving him at war with himself, as if it were he that was at the extreme left and where he wanted to be at the other end of the spectrum. He perceived his failure to be his fault and he was angry with himself.

He is long gone from the area and he did not keep in touch. I don't know what happened to him, but the memory of the conversation remains. I listened and gave him advice, drawing from my own religious vocabulary. "In Judaism, your spouse and your spirit are the same thing. There is nothing wrong with your spirit that cannot readily be mended. It is all there for you in the Ten Commandments."

Indeed, the essence of these Ten Commandments is an outward reaching spirituality, not one that is self-absorbed. Judaism is a world engaging religion; the road to spiritual truth is not taken in isolation but is outward bound. We reach spiritual truth by engaging with the world, the family, and the community. The world is a good place, the human spirit is good, and worldly pleasures are to be enjoyed with moderation and within limits. Judaism teaches a unity of the spirit and the world.

We take this path as outlined by the Ten Commandments and explained by bar Hiyya and his colleagues. We learned that we cannot control our thoughts, but we can integrate our thinking and our doing. Speaking depends on nuance and is a way of engaging with family and community. With family we saw the reasonable approach of honoring parents, community, caring for the weak, protection of the stranger. God is more than just a matter of reward and punishment; we aspire to the godlike by asserting the primacy of time over space and being over having, as well as by making ends and means consistent. In following this proscription of the Ten Commandments, we strive for an ideal life and society The Ten Commandments, as explained by a little known teacher, determine how our thoughts, speech, and actions engage with the world.